SOCCER

about the author

Dr. Richard L. Nelson is Department Chairman and Professor of Health and Physical Education at Miami University, Oxford, Ohio. He earned his B.S. in Education and the Master of Arts degrees at the Ohio State University and his Doctorate of Education degree at the University of Cincinnati.

Dr. Nelson's professional experiences include teaching at the elementary, secondary, and college levels. He was physical education and intramural director at Hamilton High School, Hamilton, Ohio, from 1953-1956. He has been teaching health and physical education at Miami University for the past twenty-three years. Soccer classes are among the many activities that he has taught over the years.

As a member and officer of numerous professional organizations, Dr. Nelson has engaged in a wide variety of professional activities related to health and physical education. He has published articles concerning soccer, gymnastics, and bowling. He has served as co-director for an Ohio State Department of Education Drug and Health Educaton Project and the Metropolitan Health Planning Corporation, Cleveland, Ohio, Dental Health Project.

SOCCER
Fourth Edition

Physical Education Activities Series

Richard L. Nelson
Miami University, Oxford, Ohio

Cover photo by Max Winter

Illustrations by Milton M. Myers

Photography by James L. Morner

Photographs of Mark Smith, Steven Frederick, and Maryanne Guiney

wcb

Wm. C. Brown Company Publishers
Dubuque, Iowa

Consulting Editors

Physical Education
Aileene Lockhart
Texas Woman's University

Parks and Recreation
David Gray
California State University, Long Beach

Health
Robert Kaplan
The Ohio State University

**Physical Education Activities
Evaluation Materials Editor**

Jane A. Mott
Texas Woman's University

Copyright © 1966, 1967, 1971, 1976, 1981 by
Wm. C. Brown Company Publishers

Library of Congress Catalog Card Number: 80-66358

ISBN 0-697-07094-8

Printed in the United States of America

contents

preface

The purpose of this book is to provide men and women with information regarding one of the world's most popular team sports—soccer. It is a vigorous game that demands skill, endurance, teamwork, and fast thinking.

The fourth edition possesses numerous improvements that should enable both students and teachers to find the book more useable and more meaningful in the instructional setting. Significant changes occur in chapter organization and a new chapter on goalkeeping skills is included. Rules of the game, facts for enthusiasts, references, and resources are updated. In the Appendix there is a generous supply of test questions with accompanying answers. These questions have been carefully formulated in relation to the instructional material presented in the book. They are representative of the types of questions that can be used to evaluate the knowledge, attitudes, and skills that students have attained as a result of instruction in soccer.

Prior to 1979, there was considerable variation in soccer rules for men and women. Although their rules are still not identical, the NAGWS has minimized differences. Important rule variations for women are indicated in Chapter 8. The chapters on skills and patterns of play are applicable to both men and women.

As in previous editions, these pages are not merely devoted to detailing the rules or to describing *how* to perform the fundamental skills involved in soccer although this information is included. An attempt has been made to go further; the *purpose* and *application* of skills and regulations are pointed out. In other words, it is hoped that readers will find not only the basis for a real understanding of the sport, but also may accelerate their progress and self-confidence, and, consequently, their satisfaction by applying the suggestions that are made for practice and by bearing in mind principles that will aid in the development of offensive and defensive strategy.

Self-evaluation questions are distributed throughout the text. These afford readers typical examples of the kinds of understanding and levels of skill that they should be acquiring as they progress toward mastery of soccer. Students should not only answer the printed questions, but should pose additonal ones as a self-check on learning. Since the order in which the content of the text is read and the teaching progression of the instructor are matters of individual decision, the evaluative materials are not positioned according to the presentation of given topics. In some instances students may find that they cannot respond fully and accurately to a question until they have read more extensively or have gained more playing experience. From time to time they should return to such troublesome questions until they are sure of the answers or have developed the skills called for, as the case may be.

Instructional objectives are listed at the beginning of each chapter. These objectives are stated in behavioral terms; that is, they state what is to be learned and what is to be evaluated according to the content of each chapter.

Although this book is designed primarily for college physical education classes, the information and purposes are appropriate for all soccer players, those in high school, recreational, intramural, and interscholastic programs.

what is soccer like?

1

The purpose of this chapter is to enable each student to—

1. compare and contrast soccer with other popular sports played in the United States,
2. name each player on a team and identify basic playing positions,
3. recognize the worldwide popularity of soccer,
4. recognize each of the markings on the field of play.

In contrast to most games played in the United States, soccer is played primarily with the feet. Other parts of the body, such as the head, chest, abdomen, thighs, and shins, are also brought into use in the performance of many of the basic skills. With the exception of the goalkeeper, however, the use of hands and arms is strictly prohibited.

The game is started at the halfway line within the center circle by means of a placekick. The game is played by two teams of eleven players who attempt to advance the ball toward the opponent's goal with the purpose of scoring a field goal by propelling the ball across the goal line, between the uprights, and under the crossbar.

Intercollegiate soccer rules divide a soccer game into two equal periods of forty-five minutes with a ten-minute intermission between halves. The game, as played by college classes, is usually divided into four quarters that are eight to ten minutes each with a one-minute intermission after the first and third quarters and a ten-minute intermission at the half.

The eleven players comprising a soccer team are named as follows: goalkeeper, right fullback, left fullback, right halfback, center halfback, left halfback, outside right, inside right, center forward, inside left, and outside left. Figure 1.1 shows a basic position of play for each team member.

Most American students find participation in soccer both very enjoyable and beneficial. To play the game well, one must develop physical stamina and excellent neuromuscular coordination, intellectual alertness and the ability to make adjustments to rapidly changing situations, emotional control and gentlemanly conduct, and social graces that promote good interpersonal relationships.

1. Goalkeeper
2. Right Fullback
3. Left Fullback
4. Right Halfback
5. Center Halfback

6. Left Halfback
7. Outside Right
8. Inside Right
9. Center Forward
10. Inside Left
11. Outside Left

Fig. 1.1

Soccer is often called the "universal game." What baseball is to the United States, soccer is to the rest of the world. It is difficult to determine how many millions of people play the game, but it is estimated that the number of fans may reach over 600 million. In many parts of the world (Europe and Latin America, for example) crowds of 100,000 or more at a single match are not uncommon. In Brazil a stadium built solely for soccer games seats 200,000 spectators! The game is played in more than 130 nations and enjoys a long history.

Within the United States, soccer has undergone tremendous growth since World War II. The game is played extensively in the East, South, Midwest, and Far West. It is played on a competitive basis in hundreds of schools, colleges, and amateur clubs. There are over seven hundred college and three thousand secondary school teams playing soccer in the United States.

As in most other sports, the skills of soccer can be practiced in an area of any size and on almost any type surface. To play the game, however, an area the size of a football field or larger is required. Within the boundaries of the official field (110 to 120 by 65 to 75 yards for men and 100 to 110 by 60 to 70 yards for women) are goalposts with attached nets and numerous markings, including goal areas, penalty areas, corner-kick areas, penalty marks, and a center circle (fig. 1.1).

the language and lore of soccer

2

The purpose of this chapter is to enable each student to—

1. become familiar with the historical development and present status of soccer as a national and international sport,
2. conclude that soccer is a worldwide sport that is gaining enthusiastic support in the United States,
3. define the meanings of terms that are peculiar to soccer.

Sports in the United States are the result of an infinite number of influences. A great many of our present sports, including soccer, are not American in origin. Soccer, or a game resembling it, is the oldest team sport in written history. The ancient Greeks played a type of soccer called harpaston. The Romans adopted the game and later introduced it into England. The English version of soccer is considered by many historians to be the origin of the game we know today.

As might be suspected, the game of soccer that became popular with the common people of England had many severe limitations as a sport. Lack of rules, regulations, and general organization led to destruction of property, serious injuries, and loss of life. Consequently, English aristocrats opposed the game, and numerous monarchs outlawed it down through the years. Not until the early seventeenth century was soccer sanctioned by King James I. By 1700 the game was adopted and modified by many English schools, colleges, and clubs.

In the first quarter of the nineteenth century, running with the ball was introduced at Rugby School. This development led to the differentiation now made between soccer and football. By the 1830s soccer was played in American colleges under varied rules. During the 1860s the London Football Association was formed in England. This association determined the rules and regulations that governed the game of soccer.

In America, Rutgers and Princeton Universities played the first intercollegiate soccer game in 1869. A continued lack of uniformity in rules finally led to the formation of the Intercollegiate Association Football League during the early 1900s. This organization functioned until 1925. Soccer became a part of the Olympic Games in 1900 and has remained quite popular over the years.

The United States Football Association, which was founded in 1913, was accepted in affiliation with the Federation Internationale de Football Association in 1914. In 1945 the name was changed to the United States Soccer Football Association (USSFA). The Intercollegiate Soccer Football Association of America became an active member of the USSFA in 1926.

The USSFA organized tournament play for the National (Open) Challenge Cup in 1913. Originally this tournament was for amateur play only, but today it is open to all professional and amateur teams in the United States. It is soccer's most coveted award in this country. In 1922 the need for a separate award for amateur teams became evident. As a result, the USSFA established the National Amateur Challenge Cup, which is a tournament for amateur teams only.

The Jules Rimet trophy, or World Cup, which was established in 1930, is the emblem of world supremacy in soccer. To the soccer world, the World Cup tournament is like the Olympic Games; and it occurs every four years midway between the Olympic years. It is commonly called the World Series of sport since soccer teams from most of the countries in the world compete in the tournament.

Past winners of the World Cup include Uruguay, Italy, West Germany, Brazil, and England. Prior to 1970, Uruguay, Italy, and Brazil had won the world championship twice. According to the rules, the team that wins the cup three times gains permanent possession of it, although world championship matches will continue to be played. In the 1970 World Cup tournament all three teams advanced to the semifinals with Brazil defeating Italy for the world soccer title and permanent possession of the Jules Rimet Cup. The 1978 World Cup Championship, which was held in Argentina, was of interest to millions of soccer fans. In fact, it has been estimated that one billion radio and television fans throughout the world listened to or watched Argentina defeat the Netherlands by a score of three to one.

Within recent years there has been greater interest in soccer in the United States. The International Soccer League (ISL), which was formed in 1960, brought international championship teams to play games in many of the larger cities of the United States. It has been estimated that in its first five years of operation the ISL had a total attendance of over one million people. This league ceased to function after 1965. Past exhibition games between outstanding international teams have drawn record-breaking crowds ranging from twenty-eight thousand to over forty thousand fans for a single game.

In 1967 the organization of two professional soccer leagues in the United States further increased interest and enthusiasm for the game. The United Soccer Association, which was recognized by the USSFA and FIFA, organized a twelve-team league. The National Professional Soccer League, which was not recognized by the USSFA or the FIFA, organized a ten-team league. Both of these leagues played scheduled league games during 1967. However, dwindling attendance (average attendance was five thousand per game)

Can you recall when the last World Cup competition was held and who won the trophy? When will the next competition be held?

caused financial problems. The two leagues merged to become the North American Soccer League (NASL) in 1968, and the league consisted of five professional teams in 1969. Within the last few years soccer interest in the United States has been increasing. The NASL disclosed that figures for the 1974 opening games revealed a vast improvement in attendance. In 1975 there were twenty teams in the league and in 1978 there were twenty-four teams. Attendance increased by over one million from 1977 to 1978. The NASL entered a United States soccer team in World Cup regional competition in 1978. Unfortunately, the team was not strong enough to advance to the final field of sixteen teams that competed for the World Cup Championship.

SOCCER TERMS

Charging   A method of unbalancing the player who has possession or is attempting to gain possession of the ball.

Clearing   A throw or kick by the goalkeeper who has stopped a ball in the vicinity of the goal area.

Corner Kick   A kick made by the attacking team from a corner arc. A corner kick is awarded when the ball is last touched by a defensive player and passes over the goal line without resulting in a goal.

Cross   A ball kicked from one side of the field to the other side.

Dangerous Play   Play that is likely to cause injury. Raising the foot shoulder-high, attempting to head a ball below waist level, or executing a double kick within six feet of a player, for example, constitute dangerous play.

Direct Free Kick   A free kick from which a goal can be scored directly. It is awarded for personal fouls and major infractions of the rules.

Dribbling   A method of advancing the ball with the feet by a series of short taps.

Drop Ball   A ball held by the referee and allowed to fall directly to the ground between two opponents. The ball is in play when it touches the ground. A goal may be scored directly from a drop ball.

Feint Movements   Movements of the body, especially the knees and feet, made for the purpose of deceiving your opponent as to your real intention.

Goal   A one-point score occuring when the ball passes wholly over the goal line, between the goalposts, and under the crossbar.

Goal Kick   An indirect free kick made by any defending player from the goal box. A goal kick is awarded when the ball is last touched by an offensive player and passes over the goal line without resulting in a goal.

Goalkeeper   A player designated to guard the goal. The "goalie" may run with the ball and touch it with the hands under specified conditions; these are special privileges that no other player enjoys.

Handling   The act of carrying, striking, or propelling the ball with the hand or arm.

Heading   A method of passing, scoring, or bringing the ball under control by allowing it to come in contact with the forehead.

Immunity   The goalkeeper may not be charged in the penalty area. While the goalie has possession of the ball, an opponent may not interfere in any manner.

Indirect Free Kick   A free kick from which a goal cannot be scored until the ball is touched by another player. It is awarded for technical and minor infractions of the rules.

Instep   The top portion of the foot covered by the shoelace.

Instep Kick   A long kick performed by making contact with the ball at the instep or shoelace.

Kickoff   A place kick from the center spot within the center circle that puts the ball into play at the beginning of each quarter and after each score. The kickoff rule specifies conditions of play.

Loft or Lob   A high, soft kick.

Marking   Guarding or covering the players with the ball when they move into your area of play.

Obstruction   A method of blocking the path an opponent wishes to take when you are not playing the ball.

Penalty Box   That area directly in front of the mouth of the goal (eighteen by forty-five yards). The goalkeeper may use the hands in this area only.

Penalty Kick   A direct free kick from a spot (penalty mark) twelve yards from the goal line. It is awarded to the offended team for fouls committed by the defensive team in its own penalty area.

Save   A shot at the goal that is stopped by the goalkeeper.

Tackling   A method of gaining possession of the ball by use of the feet. Unnecessary roughness and use of the hands are not permitted.

Throw-In   A two-handed, over-the-head throw that puts the ball into play after it has gone out of play over a touchline.

Touchline   The boundary lines on each side of the field.

Unintentional Handling   The ball touches the hands or arms of a player. No penalty is awarded even if the offending team gains an advantage.

Volleying   Kicking the ball while it is in the air.

playing the game
3

The purpose of this chapter is to enable each student to—

1. locate various places in his community where soccer is played,
2. identify newspapers and magazines that publish articles about soccer.

Learning to play soccer represents a distinct challenge to most Americans since most of our sports place emphasis upon eye-hand coordination. Once that basic skills and knowledges of the unique game of soccer are learned, however, interest and enthusiasm in it spread rapidly. Undoubtedly, soccer is played in many places in your community. It is generally played in the public schools in physical education classes, in intramural programs, and in interscholastic programs. It is also played in recreation programs and camps. There has been phenomenal growth of youth soccer in the United States within recent years. It was estimated that the American Youth Soccer Organization included over 250,000 youngsters by 1978.

If there is a college or university in or near your community, the chances are good that you can see soccer played in classes, intramurally, and interscholastically. You can also see soccer games in cities that have amateur and professional soccer teams. In addition, you can watch professional and international soccer games on television.

You can read about soccer in the sports pages of many newspapers. *Soccer America* and *Soccer World* are weekly publications devoted to soccer. Popular magazines such as *Time, Newsweek, Reader's Digest, Sports Illustrated* and other sports magazines occasionally publish articles about soccer.

If you are interested in soccer from the teaching or coaching point of view, the *Athletic Journal* and the *Scholastic Coach* publish numerous articles. Also available are a monthly publication by the United States Soccer Football Association entitled *Soccer News* and a quarterly publication by the National Soccer Coaches of America entitled *Soccer Journal*.

Soccer tournaments are generally of either the single elimination or the round-robin type. In most schools and colleges, the round-robin type of tournament is popular. This type of tournament places the teams in leagues; each team in the league plays every other team in that league. At the end of league play, the winner is determined on the basis of percentage points and, in some cases, a single elimination tournament among the league leaders to determine the championship.

skills essential for everyone

4

The purpose of this chapter is to enable each student to—

1. identify general principles that apply to learning each of the skills of soccer,
2. synthesize information pertaining to the proper execution of each of the skills,
3. analyze the game situations in which each of the skills may be useful.

SKILLS AND TECHNIQUES OF KICKING

There are two groups of kicks to be mastered in soccer. The first group consists of long kicks such as the instep kick, outside of the foot kick, and volley kicks. The second group is composed of short kicks such as the push pass, lob, and flick kick.

General Information Concerning Kicking

1. Determine the direction and distance you want the ball to travel.
2. Keep your eyes on the ball at all times.
3. Learn the techniques of the kicks on a stationary or slow-moving ball.
4. Your body, especially your kicking leg, should be relaxed.
5. Use your arms to help maintain balance.
6. Practice kicking skills and techniques with both feet.
7. Long kicks generally travel distances greater than fifteen yards.

Instep Kick   The instep kick, if executed properly, will enable you to kick the ball with both power and accuracy. It can be used effectively on ground balls and bouncing balls. The instep kick is especially advantageous in scoring, free-kick, and passing situations. To perform an instep kick:

1. Place the nonkicking foot four to six inches to the side of the ball.
2. Flex the knee of the kicking foot until it blocks the ball from your view.
3. Straighten the knee as it moves over the ball and swing the leg from the hip.

Fig. 4.1   Instep kick

4. Keep the toe pointed down. The top portion of the foot covered by the shoelace or the inside portion of the instep should contact the ball slightly below its midpoint.
5. To keep the ball low lean forward from the waist as your foot meets the ball. Moving your arms backward and upward will help you maintain balance.
6. To loft the ball, place the nonkicking foot six to eight inches to the side of and slightly behind the ball. Lean your body backward as your foot meets the ball. Moving your arms forward and upward will help you maintain balance.
7. Follow through by continuing the upward swing of your leg (fig. 4.1).

Using an instep kick on a stationary ball, can you send a ground ball directly to a partner standing 20 yards away 6 times out of 10 tries? 8 out of 10? 10 out of 10? Can you do the same lofting the ball?

Outside of the Foot Kick   This kick is the same as the instep kick except that the toe is turned inward. It enables you to kick a fast, low curved ball with sideward spin. It is an effective means of shooting around an opponent because of the long arc which the ball travels. It is also valuable when used as a corner kick. (See instep kick for points related to the performance of this skill.)

Volleying   The volley and half-volley kicks are executed while the ball is in the air. When executing a volley, the ball is kicked while it is in the air, either before or after it bounces (fig. 4.2). The half-volley is performed by kicking the ball just after it strikes the ground (fig. 4.3). The volley kick will yield a

Fig. 4.2   Volley kick

Fig. 4.3   Half-volley kick

rather high, lofting ball, while the half-volley kick will produce a relatively low ball. To perform either:

1. Swing the kicking leg forward from the hip. Keep the knee flexed and the toe pointed down.
2. Contact the ball slightly below its midpoint with the instep or shoelace.
3. Follow through by continuing the upward swing of the leg.
4. Kick the ball while it is in the air to loft it; kick the ball near the ground to keep it low.

Stand on the penalty kick mark. As your partner tosses the ball to you from between the goal posts, can you consistently kick volleys over the crossbar and half-volleys under the bar?

Pivot Instep Kick   The pivot instep kick has the distinct advantage of enabling you to change the direction of the ball. In essence, the ball will travel at right angles to your approach. This kick is used on ground balls only; it is particularly effective for corner kicks and in scoring situations. To perform a pivot instep kick:

1. Place the nonkicking foot no more than eighteen inches behind and slightly to the inside of the ball.
2. Swing the kicking leg forward from the hip, keeping the knee slightly flexed and the toe pointed down.
3. Pivot on the nonkicking foot as the kicking leg swings forward.

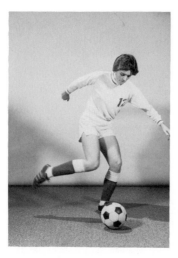

Fig. 4.4   Pivot instep kick

4. Contact the ball slightly below its midpoint with the shoelace.
5. Follow through by continuing the upward swing of the leg (fig. 4.4).
6. Lean forward and work for forward spin on the ball in order to keep the ball low.

Inside of the Foot Kicks   The push pass and lob are excellent kicks to use for short passes and goal shots. Although these kicks are useful in maintaining control of the ball, they are not very deceptive. To perform inside of the foot kicks:

1. Swing the kicking leg forward from the hip with the knee slightly flexed and the toe pointed down and out.
2. Straighten the leg as the inside of the foot contacts the ball.
3. To perform the push pass, push the ball with the inside of the foot without causing it to bounce (fig. 4.5).
4. To perform the lob, place the inside of the foot slightly under the ball, lift your foot as you kick, and lean your body backward (fig. 4.6).

Outside of the Foot Kick   The flick or jab kick is used for short passes and dribbling. Feint movements executed before the pass is attempted make it difficult to intercept. To perform the flick kick:

1. Swing the kicking leg away from your body with the knee slightly flexed and the toe pointed down and in.
2. As the outside of the foot contacts the ball, straighten the leg.
3. Try to jab the ball with the outside of the foot and follow through with a slight outward movement of the entire leg (fig. 4.7).
4. To raise the ball off the ground, place the outside of the foot slightly under the ball and pull the ankle upward.

Fig. 4.5   Push pass

Fig. 4.6   Lob pass

Fig. 4.7   The flick kick or jab

Partners face each other about fifteen yards apart. Can you pass the ball back and forth six times without losing control? Can you do the same at twenty yards? at twenty-five yards?

Fig. 4.8   Side of foot volley

Side of Foot Volley   This type of volley is used for short accurate kicks and for maintaining control of the ball. It is used when the ball is approximately knee-high or lower. To perform the side of the foot volley:

1. Flex the kicking leg at the hip and the knee so that the knee points sideward and the foot turns outward.
2. Swing the kicking leg forward from the hip.
3. Contact the ball slightly below its midpoint with the side of the foot (fig. 4.8).
4. Follow through by continuing the forward swing of the leg.

Sole of Foot and Heel Kicks   In general, these kicks are difficult for beginners in soccer. Nevertheless, they are good backward passes and provide a means of stopping a rolling ball. In executing both kicks, it is essential that you know where you are passing. These kicks are more difficult if the ball is rolling and you are running. Practice and good judgment will eliminate stepping on the ball. To succeed with these kicks:

1. Place the nonkicking foot to the side of the ball.
2. Keep the knee of the kicking foot flexed until the ball is under your body.
3. To execute the sole of the foot kick, place the sole of the foot lightly on the ball and kick the ball behind you by flexing the knee (fig. 4.9).
4. To execute the heel kick, hit the ball in the center with your heel as you swing the leg backward from the hip (fig. 4.10).

Fig. 4.9   Sole of the foot kick   Fig. 4.10   Heel kick

SKILLS AND TECHNIQUES OF CONTROL

The process of bringing the ball under your control is called trapping. Trapping is more than just stopping a ball; a trap may bring a ball to the ground, change its direction, or slow it down. The method by which you trap the ball will be determined by your skill and also will depend upon game conditions. In general, a trap is successful when you have intercepted the ball and are ready to dribble, pass, or kick it.

General Information Concerning Trapping

1. Keep your eyes on the ball at all times.
2. Learn the techniques of trapping first on slow-moving balls.
3. Maintain a relaxed body throughout the performance of the skill.

Sole of the Foot Trap   The sole of the foot can be used to trap a rolling or bouncing ball. Although this trap is simple to perform, its effectiveness is decreased as running speed is increased. To trap the ball with the sole of the foot:

1. Extend the trapping leg forward with the foot four to five inches away from the ground and at a forty-five-degree angle to it.
2. Allow the ball to roll into the trap formed by your foot and the ground (fig. 4.11).

Fig. 4.11   Sole of the foot trap

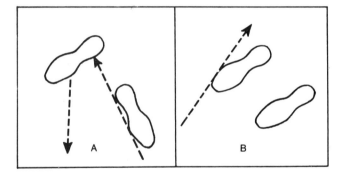

Fig. 4.12

Side of the Foot Trap   The inside or outside of the foot may be used to deflect the ball and, thereby, enable you to gain control of it. This type of trap is used by all players except for the goalkeeper, since it would be risky to deflect the ball toward the goal. To trap the ball with the side of the foot:

1. Flex the knee of the trapping leg, raising the foot off the ground three to four inches.
2. Turn the foot out when deflecting the ball with the inside of the foot.
3. Turn the foot in when deflecting the ball with the outside of the foot.
4. The body should lean in the direction the ball is to go (fig. 4.12).

Fig. 4.13   Inside of the thigh trap

Inside of the Thigh Trap   An excellent method of gaining control of a ball in low flight is to allow it to strike the relaxed muscles of the thigh. The fleshy part of the leg absorbing the impact of the ball will cause it to drop near your feet. To trap the ball in this manner:

1. Shift your body weight to the nontrapping leg.
2. Bend the knee of the trapping leg at a right angle to the line of flight of the ball with the foot off the ground.
3. As the ball strikes the thigh, a slight backward movement of the leg from the hip will help absorb the impact and will cause the ball to drop at your feet (fig. 4.13).

Stomach and Chest Traps   These traps are used when the ball is traveling above the ground at the appropriate height, i.e., either abdomen or chest height. In either case:

1. Relax and bend forward at the waist as the ball strikes your body.
2. Extend your arms away from your body.
3. Jump off both feet and allow your body to "give" in order to absorb the impact of a hard-kicked ball.
4. Move forward in the desired direction as the ball hits your body (fig. 4.14).

Which way should the foot be turned as you trap the ball with the inside of the foot? With the outside of the foot? Can you trap the ball successfully with either foot or leg?

Fig. 4.14   Stomach (or chest) trap

SKILLS AND TECHNIQUES OF PASSING

Passing refers to kicking the ball to a teammate. As in any other team game, good passing and pass receiving are of the utmost importance. In soccer the passer and the receiver have well-defined responsibilities. You must be sure you can pass the ball without its being intercepted. You should pass only to a teammate who is not marked (guarded), and you must be able to judge distances with some degree of accuracy. You also must be capable of kicking the ball with enough skill so that the receiver can gain control of it. The receiver, on the other hand, must work to be in position to receive the ball. Thus, the receiver should move between any opposing player and the passer, must be ready to receive a pass at all times, must keep the eyes on the ball, and must go to meet the ball once it is on its way. Remember, a good pass is the key to team play.

Passing may be accomplished by any of the long or short kicks previously discussed. Heading (to be discussed later) may also be used as a means of passing the ball. In general, it is best to loft the ball on long passes. Game situations and weather conditions, however, will help determine when to pass the ball low or high.

General Information Concerning Passing

1. Use a form of the instep kick for long passes.
2. Use the inside of the foot, the outside of the foot, or the head for short passes.
3. Time your pass with the speed of the receiver.
4. Devote all of your attention to your passing.

When passing:

1. Look at your receiver before kicking.
2. Look at the ball while in the act of kicking.
3. Lead the receiver; i.e., pass so that the ball will be in front of the receiver.
4. Use feint movements whenever possible to deceive your opponent.

Can you dribble a ball without losing control of it for 20 yards? 30 yards? 50 yards? Can you dribble in a circle? Can you dribble in a figure 8 pattern?

SKILLS AND TECHNIQUES OF DRIBBLING

Dribbling is a method of advancing the ball by a series of short taps with the feet. The basic purpose of the dribble is to maintain possession of the ball. The dribble is used most effectively when you are not closely guarded (marked) by an opponent, when there are no unguarded teammates to whom you may pass, when you are attempting to set up a play, and when you want to maneuver for a more advantageous passing or scoring position. A simple rule to follow is to pass the ball rather than dribble whenever possible. An unnecessary dribble increases your chances of losing the ball.

General Information Concerning Dribbling

1. The ball should be kept near the feet throughout the dribble.
2. Push or tap rather than kick the ball.
3. Work for ball control rather than speed.
4. Advanced tactics such as swerving, feigning, and changing of pace make dribbling much more effective.

Inside of the Foot Dribble   This method of dribbling gives best ball control. Use the dribble only when there is no better alternative; a good pass will produce better results in your team effort to defeat an opponent. To dribble with the inside of the foot:

1. Slightly flex the knee of one leg, raising the foot three to four inches off the ground.
2. Push the ball straight ahead with the inside of your foot.
3. Keep your body forward and keep your head over the ball.
4. Step forward, shifting the body weight to the dribbling leg, and repeat the movements with the other foot (fig. 4.15).

Outside of Foot Dribble   This type of dribbling is used when attempting to keep your body between an opponent and the ball. The ball is dribbled with the same foot every other step. Although this method of dribbling gives greater

Fig. 4.15   Inside of the foot dribble

Fig. 4.16   Outside of the foot dribble

speed, it is difficult to execute and decreases ball control. To dribble with the outside of the foot:

1. Slightly flex the knee of one leg, raising the foot three to four inches off the ground.
2. Push the ball straight ahead with the outside of the foot.
3. Keep the body weight forward with the head over the ball.
4. Step forward, shifting the body weight to the dribbling leg. Continue the forward motion by stepping through with the opposite leg, repeating the movements with the dribbling leg (fig. 4.16).

SKILLS AND TECHNIQUES OF THROWING IN

The technique of the throw-in is governed basically by the throw-in rule. You must face the field of play and must have part of each foot either on the touchline or on the ground outside the touchline at the moment of delivering the ball. You must use both hands and must deliver the ball from overhead.

The throw-in is important not only because it is a method of restarting play, but also because it is a way of initiating offensive play.

When throwing in the ball, where should you aim in relation to the receiver? Why?

General Information Concerning Throwing In

1. Assume a comfortable, balanced stance with the feet either slightly apart or one foot ahead of the other. A few running steps may be taken if desired.
2. Try to conceal the direction of the throw until the last moment.
3. Lead the receiver; i.e., throw the ball so that it will be in front of the player.

Throwing with One Foot in Advance of the Other   This method has the advantage of enabling you to bend the body backwards and maintain balance. Consequently, a more powerful throw can be executed due to the longer forward sweep of the trunk and arms. As with any method of delivering the throw, care must be taken to keep a portion of both feet on the ground.

1. Place your hands on opposite sides of the ball with the fingers comfortably spread.
2. Place one foot approximately four to six inches ahead of the other.
3. As you shift your body weight to the rear leg, take the ball over and well behind your head and bend your body backwards. Keep the heels slightly off the ground (fig. 4.17).
4. As you initiate the throw, transfer your weight from the rear leg to the front leg.
5. The wrists, elbows, shoulders, and trunk muscles are used in executing the throw.
6. Follow through by extending the arms, wrists, and fingers forward in front of the body.

Fig. 4.17   Throwing with one foot in advance of the other

There are three reasons for heading a ball. Do you know what they are?

SKILLS AND TECHNIQUES OF HEADING

The skill of heading consists of bringing the ball under control by means of the head. Thus, when you use your head physically, you are also using it mentally. Heading can be used as a method of passing the ball, scoring a goal, or bringing the ball to the ground.

For reasons of safety, a number of factors must be kept in mind when heading. First, you cannot push off or climb up an opponent for the purpose of heading. Second, you should never charge an opponent who is in the air heading the ball. Third, you should never create a "dangerous play" by heading a ball lower than waist height. (Similarly, you should never kick at a ball higher than shoulder height.)

General Information Concerning Heading

1. The best type of heading directs the ball to the ground (to your feet or a teammate's feet).
2. Use your entire upper body to obtain speed and power.
3. Keep your eyes on the ball until it meets your forehead.
4. Keep your eyes open throughout the performance of the skill.
5. Jump up to meet the ball.

To head the ball:

1. Jump off the ground in order to meet the ball in the air.
2. While in the air use your arms to maintain balance.
3. Bend your body backward at the waist and use your neck muscles to direct the ball forcefully to the ground.
4. The midpoint of the ball should make contact with your forehead at the hairline.
5. Stiffen your neck and throw your head at the ball.
6. To head the ball to the side, meet the ball with the side of your forehead and thrust your head to the side (fig. 4.18).

Repeatedly head the ball 15 to 18 inches above your head. For how many contacts can you keep the ball airborne?

SKILLS AND TECHNIQUES OF CHARGING AND TACKLING

Charging is a method of unbalancing an opponent who has possession, or is attempting to secure possession, of the ball. A fair charge consists of a nudge or a contact with your near shoulder. When charging, both players must be in an upright position and within playing distance of the ball. In addition, both players must have at least one foot on the ground and their arms held close to their bodies. The charge must not be violent and cannot be made from behind unless your opponent is intentionally obstructing.

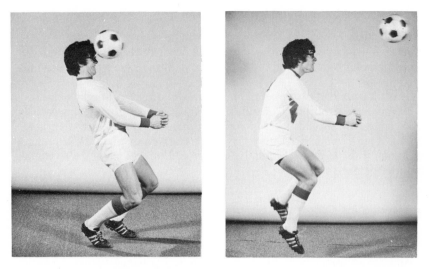

Fig. 4.18   Heading the ball

Tackling is a method of gaining possession of the ball by use of the feet. A tackle is also considered successful if you force the dribbler to make a poor pass or to lose control of the ball. More often than not, tackling and charging are used in concert.

General Information Concerning Charging and Tackling

1. Watch your opponent for swerving and feint tactics and recognize these for what they are: attempts to fool you.
2. Do not charge and tackle until your opponent has moved in a given direction with the ball.
3. Do not charge violently; govern the force of the charge according to the speed at which you and your opponent are traveling.
4. Make every attempt to gain possession of the ball rather than just "bumping" your opponent.

One-Leg Tackle   This type of tackle is used head on, from the side, or from the rear. To tackle an approaching opponent with one leg:

1. Nudge your opponent's shoulder with your right shoulder and place the inside of your right foot against the ball (fig. 4.19).
2. Trap the ball with your right foot and leg.
3. Push the ball forward with your right foot and step forward with your left leg.
4. Perform the sole of the foot tackle by trapping the ball between your foot and the ground.
5. Perform the two-leg tackle by placing both feet in front of the ball with the heels close together. Turn your knees outward and lean your body forward. Trap the ball between your legs as the shoulder charge is made.

Fig. 4.19   Charging and tackling

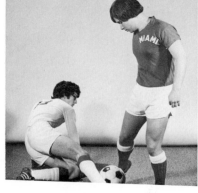

Fig. 4.20   Sliding tackle

Sliding Tackle   This is a difficult skill for men to perform and can lead to a dangerous play situation if it is executed improperly. According to women's rules, it is an infraction, i.e., it is considered an attempt to trip the opponent. Beginning and intermediate players should not attempt to hook the ball away from a dribbler in this manner since it is dangerous. Moreover, it forces the tackler to the ground and eliminates him from further play on the ball. To perform the sliding tackle:

1. Initiate the slide to the ground by flexing the knee of the leg closest to the ground (fig. 4.20).

2. Contact the ground with the leg, thigh, and/or buttock.
3. Maintain balance by placing the hand on the sliding side of the body on the ground. Keep your elbow flexed.
4. Extend the takeoff leg forward toward the ball in an attempt to hook it with the instep of the foot (fig. 4.20).

goalkeeping skills
5

The purpose of this chapter is to enable each student to—

1. identify general principles that apply to learning goalkeeping skills,
2. recognize goalkeeping skills and examine their purposes and execution,
3. analyze goalkeeping situations and determine when each of the skills is most applicable.

The goalkeeper position is unique in that the goalie has the privilege of using the hands in the penalty area. As goalie, you may catch, carry, strike, or propel the ball with the hands or arms. Moreover, an opponent may not impede your progress in any manner while you have possession of the ball. There are two groups of goalkeeping skills to be perfected in soccer. The first group includes fielding skills, such as catching, tipping, and punching the ball and diving for the ball. The second group consists of distribution (clearing) techniques such as throwing, rolling, and kicking the ball. Positional play and strategy for the goalkeeper are discussed in Chapter Seven.

General Information Concerning Goalkeeping Skills

1. Place your body directly in front of the ball whenever possible.
2. Keep your eyes on the ball at all times.
3. Catch the ball when possible; strike or punch the ball for difficult clearance or to hit the ball out-of-bounds.
4. Use two hands when catching the ball and keep the thumbs and fingers spread apart.
5. After collecting the ball, move to either side of the goal area to clear it.

What is the first action the goalkeeper should take as the ball approaches?

Fig. 5.1   Collecting the ball

Fielding Or Collecting The Ball   There are basically three types of balls to field in soccer—the ground ball, the chest high ball and the ball in the air. To collect a ground ball:

1. Keep your body directly in front of the ball.
2. Keep your eyes on the ball until it is in your hands.
3. Spread your feet four to six inches apart and bend forward at waist with the knees straight (fig. 5.1).
4. Hold your hands two to three inches apart, turn the palms forward with the fingers pointing down, spread the fingers apart, and keep the elbows in close to the sides of the body (fig. 5.1).
5. As the ball rolls up your palms and forearms, bring it into the chest with the hands covering the ball.

To collect a chest high ball:

1. Keep your body directly in front of the ball.
2. Keep your eyes on the ball until it is in your hands.
3. Spread your feet four to six inches apart (fig. 5.2).
4. Hold your hands so that your thumbs and index fingers form a "W" with the palms forward and the fingers pointing upward. Spread the fingers apart and keep the elbows in close to the sides of the body (fig. 5.3).
5. Bring the ball into the chest and cover the ball with the hands. Keep the elbows close to each other while securing the ball into the chest.

To collect a ball in the air:

1. Keep your eyes on the ball until it is in your hands.
2. Jump upward to meet the ball. Use a one foot takeoff with the front leg flexed at the hip and knee (fig. 5.4).
3. Catch the ball at the highest point possible.

Fig. 5.2 Collecting a chest high ball

Fig. 5.3 "W" hand position

Fig. 5.4 Collecting an air ball

4. Hold the hands two to three inches apart, turn the palms forward with the fingers pointing upward and spread apart.
5. Bring the ball into the chest and cover the ball with the hands.

Tipping The Ball A method of deflecting the ball over the crossbar or to the sides of the uprights is essential when the ball cannot be caught. To tip the ball:

1. Jump upward to meet the ball.
2. Keep your eyes on the ball until the hand makes contact.
3. The tip is usually made with one hand, depending upon the situation.

Fig. 5.5   Tipping the ball   Fig. 5.6   Punching the ball

4. Spread the fingers and thumb apart; wrist and finger movements deflect the ball the desired direction (fig. 5.5).
5. If possible, deflect balls to your right with the left hand and balls to your left with the right hand.

Punching The Ball   Punching the ball with the fists is a method of deflecting it away from the goal area. This technique is used when there are other players in the immediate area who may attempt to head the ball and possibly prevent a successful catch. To punch the ball:

1. Jump upward and forward to meet the ball. Use a one foot takeoff with the front leg flexed at the hip and knee (fig. 5.6).
2. Keep your eyes on the ball until your fists make contact with it.
3. Bring both fists from the chest by extending the arms at the elbows. Punch through the ball (fig. 5.6).
4. Beginning goalkeepers should punch the ball forward and upward.

Diving For The Ball   Leaving the ground in an effort to reach the ball is risky for the inexperienced goalkeeper since maintaining or returning to a proper defensive position is difficult. The inexperienced goalkeeper should use this skill only as a last resort. Diving from a kneeling position should be mastered before attempting a standing or running dive. To perform a dive:

1. Keep your eyes on the ball.
2. Begin the dive from the basic stance, a crossover step or a side step, depending upon the situation.
3. Position the arms, waist, hips and legs so that you land on the *side* of the body and roll (fig. 5.7).

Fig. 5.7   Diving for the ball

Fig. 5.8   Rolling the ball

4. Place your lower hand behind the ball and your upper hand on top of the ball. Allow the ball to strike the ground and provide a "third hand" for better control.
5. Bring the ball to your chest, regain a standing position and move to either side of the goal area before clearing it.

Clearing or Distributing the Ball   As goalkeeper, you must decide upon a plan of action for clearing the ball after you catch it. You may roll, throw, or kick the ball to a teammate. Regardless of the method of distributing the ball, you should move to either side of the goal area first. To roll the ball to either side of the goal:

1. Bend forward at the waist with the legs spread apart and the knees slightly flexed (fig. 5.8).
2. Push the ball forward with your rear hand.
3. Step forward with your front foot, then bring your rear foot forward, keeping your body between the ball and your opponent.
4. Keep your eyes on the ball and the immediate area surrounding the ball.

To roll the ball to a teammate:

1. Hold the ball in one hand, step forward with the opposite leg and bend forward to a semi-crouch position (fig. 5.9).
2. Release the ball at ground level.
3. Time your throw (roll) with the speed of your receiver.

Fig. 5.9   Rolling the pass

Fig. 5.10   Throwing the ball

Fig. 5.11   Kicking the ball

To throw the ball to a teammate:

1. Hold the ball in one hand with the arm extended downward and to the side of the body.
2. Step forward with the opposite leg and bring the arm upward from the side of the body and over the head (fig. 5.10).
3. Release the ball when the arm reaches the head.
4. Time your throw with the speed of your receiver.

To kick the ball to a teammate:

1. Drop the ball in front of your kicking leg.
2. Swing the kicking leg forward from the hip. Keep the knee flexed and the toe pointed down (fig. 5.11).
3. Contact the ball slightly below its mid-point with the instep or shoelace.
4. Follow through by continuing the upward swing of the leg.
5. Kick the ball near the ground to keep it low.

progress can be speeded up

6

The purpose of this chapter is to enable each student to—

1. examine factors that can affect learning and explore ways to facilitate the learning of skills and knowledge,
2. identify basic instructional formations and activities for both large and small groups and describe their uses in the learning situation,
3. devise a conditioning program that will improve strength and endurance,
4. conclude that personal health and safety are important results of class instruction and participation.

Learning is a complex process. Nevertheless, there are ways to facilitate your learning of motor skills. At this point you are probably asking yourself this question: "How can I possibly remember to use all the information related to the performance and strategy of soccer?" Experience has shown that you will learn more easily and remember longer if you learn with understanding. In other words, you must not only learn the "how" of motor skills, but also the "why" and "when." As you no doubt observed in the preceding chapters, the material in this booklet is organized so that you will develop understanding. Each major technique is introduced by giving you general information that provides the specific points essential to learning the skill. Before each skill is broken down into its major components, however, its purpose and its application in game situations are discussed.

HOW TO PRACTICE

It is important to realize at the outset that if you wish to become proficient at the game of soccer, you must want to learn. There is no single aspect of learning more important than your attitude toward the game. It is a well-proved statement that practice in and of itself does not make perfect. Practice of correct movements, of course, is basic, but perfection depends upon more than mere repetition. What does lead to perfection, then, is purposiveness of practice or repetition that is active and highly motivated.

Hints for Learning

You no doubt will find the game of soccer enjoyable as you improve old skills and learn new ones. Soccer, like all other team games, requires basic skills, knowledge, and understanding that must be individually mastered and then applied to game situations in connection with teamwork. As in all learning situations, what you get out of class instruction depends entirely on you. You must be receptive to new ideas and attempt new things even though they may be different or difficult at first. You must be willing to apply yourself in learning knowledge and skills. Only through practice of basic movements beyond the point of bare mastery will you step out of the beginner's class. You must be willing to accept constructive criticism with the intention of correcting errors and misunderstandings as you become aware of them.

Check yourself on the following points to determine your progress in skill performance and team proficiency:

1. Do I understand the explanations and demonstrations of basic skills and strategies so that I have a mental picture of their execution?
2. Do I understand the purpose and application of skills and strategies in game situations?
3. Have I practiced the skills and strategies both as an individual and as a member of a small group?
4. Am I open to suggestions and corrections in learning situations?
5. Do I attempt to use new learning in game situations?

If the answers to the questions are in the affirmative, you are well on your way to improvement and success in the game of soccer.

Practice Formations for Large Classes

Since soccer is a team game, it is logical that much of your practice should be in groups. There should be at least one ball for every eight people. The following drills are designed for eight or more players. The player with the ball is designated by B; the path of the ball is represented by---; the path of the player is represented by ——; a player in formation is designated by O.

From a stationary position with the legs spread approximately fifteen to eighteen inches apart, can you smoothly top a ball back and forth from foot to foot and keep the ball on the ground? Can you alternate the speed of the ball from slow to fast and back to slow again?

Double Column   This formation is used for kicks, passes, trapping, and heading. The players in each line are spaced approximately four yards apart; the two columns are spaced approximately ten yards apart; for long kicks the two columns are spaced approximately twenty yards apart (fig. 6.1).

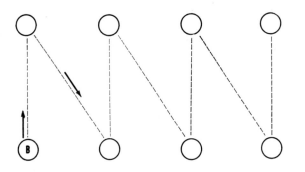

Fig. 6.1   Double column formation

Single Column   The players are spaced five yards apart in a column. One player with the ball stands in front of and faces the other players. The player with the ball dribbles in and out around the other players. As skill in dribbling is gained, the players in the column may attempt to steal the ball but must keep one foot stationary (fig. 6.2).

Fig. 6.2   Single column formation

Divided Column   The column is divided in half. Players line up in single file, each column facing the other. The player with the ball kicks it to the first player in the opposing line and goes to the end of the line. The player receiving the ball traps it, returns the ball by means of a kick, and goes to the end of the line, etc. (fig. 6.3).

Fig. 6.3   Divided column formation

Semicircle and Circle   The players form a semicircle twelve to fifteen yards in front of the goal. The player in the goalie's box can practice goalkeeper skills while the players in the semicircle practice goal shooting. Several balls can be used if kicked one after the other, not simultaneously (fig. 6.4).

Fig. 6.4   Semicircle formation

The players are spaced approximately five yards apart forming a circle. The player in the middle throws the ball to a player in the circle who heads it back, etc. The ball should be thrown fifteen to twenty feet into the air (fig. 6.5).

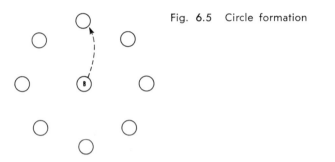

Fig. 6.5   Circle formation

Field Drills   One or two examples of field drills should enable your team to understand their organization and purpose and to devise other such drills as needed (figs. 6.6 and 6.7).

Activities for Large Groups

Many enjoyable lead-up games afford opportunities for practicing game skills and strategies. Since many of these games are relatively simple in organization, only brief descriptions of them are given.

Soccer Dodge Ball   This game is played in the same manner as regular dodge ball except that the ball must be kicked.

Circle Keep Away   The players in the circle attempt to keep the ball away from the player in the center. The arms and hands cannot be used.

Soccer Steal the Bacon   The game is played in the same manner as regular "steal the bacon" except that the ball must be dribbled.

Line Soccer   The players form two lines approximately twenty yards apart. Each line of players is assigned a number. The instructor, or an appointed leader, rolls the ball between the two lines and calls a player or players by number. Those players whose numbers are called run out to play the ball. The remaining players act as goalkeepers. The ball cannot go over the heads of the line players.

Can you kick two out of three goals from a distance of fifteen yards using the pivot instep kick to kick a stationary ball? a moving ball?

Rotate from 1 to 2, 2 to 3, 3 to 4, etc.

1—Corner Kick
2—Penalty Kick
3—Goalkeeper Skills
4—Goal Kick
5—Passing
6—Shooting
7—Goalkeeper Skills

Fig. 6.6   Field drills

Fig. 6.7   Field drills

Circle Play   The players form a circle approximately ten yards in diameter. The object of the game is to keep the ball in the air by heading or volleying it.

Dribbling Relay   One group forms a line with players spaced approximately five yards apart. Each player in the remaining group dribbles in and out of the line, attempting to maintain control of the ball.

Offensive-Defensive Situations   There are numerous variations of this activity: one-on-one situation where one offensive player attempts to out-maneuver one defensive player; two-on-one situation where two offensive players attempt to outmaneuver one defensive player; a three-on-two situation where three offensive players attempt to outmaneuver two defensive players.

Rotation Soccer   This game is played as regular soccer except that the players rotate to different positions after a specified length of time.

Half Field Play   Each team plays on one half of the field. Five players assume forward positions, and six players assume halfback, fullback, and goalkeeper positions. The forwards remain on offensive for five plays and then change to the defense.

Activities for Small Groups

There are many small group activities that will enable students to simulate game conditions more realistically. Only a few of those activities are included here. Students will find it interesting and helpful to design additional activities that will benefit them and their team.

Two-on-Two Play   Only a section of the field is used and boundaries of play are established within that section. The drill can be changed by indicating dribbling, passing, shooting, offensive play, defensive play, heading, or trapping. For example, within one-quarter of the field, two forwards play against one fullback and a goalkeeper, or within the width of the goal area from the goal line to midfield two defensive players attempt to stop two offensive players.

Three-on-Three Play   Only a section of the field is used and boundaries of play are established within that section. The drill can be changed by indicating dribbling, passing, shooting, defensive play, offensive play, heading, or trapping. For example, within one-third of the field three forwards attempt to score against two fullbacks and a goalie, or within one-half of the field three offensive players attempt to outmaneuver three defensive players.

Accuracy Drills   Place two players or one player and a marker fifteen yards apart. The object of the drill is to propel the ball to a given player, through the goal, or to a given area by means of a pass, a throw-in, a head, or a kick.

Heading Drill   Place three markers ten to fifteen yards from the touchline. Player A stands near the touchline while Player B lobs the ball into the air and calls a target number. Player A attempts to head the ball to the selected target.

Kicking Drill   This drill is especially good for goalkeepers, fullbacks, and halfbacks. Place two teams consisting of three player each on opposite touch-lines. Team A kicks the ball to Team B. Team B returns the kick from where the ball strikes the ground. The team that advances the ball over the touchline first is the winner.

Shooting Drill   Place two soccer balls two to three yards apart and about fifteen yards from the goal. Player A attempts to score by shooting one ball at the goal. Player A then shoots the second ball as quickly as possible. As skill increases, another player can roll one ball toward the shooter. The shot must then be executed on the run while the ball is moving.

Three-Player Weave   Three players form a line ready to move downfield. Player A starts play by passing the ball to the middle person, Player B. Player A then cuts behind Player B. Player B passes the ball to Player C and cuts behind. This pattern is continued throughout the drill.

Chip-Shot Drill   Three players form a triangle ready to move downfield. Player A passes the ball forward to Player B who passes the ball to Player C. Player C chips the ball over Player B's head to Player A who has moved further downfield.

Pass and Go   Three players form a triangle. Player A passes to Player B and follows the pass to assume Player B's position. Player B passes to Player C and follows the pass to assume Player C's position. This pattern is continued throughout the drill.

CONDITIONING EXERCISES

It is essential that you develop physical strength and endurance to play the game of soccer well. Strength can be defined best as the ability of the whole body or a part of the body to apply force. By increasing strength, it is then possible to increase muscular power that is a combination of strength and speed. Endurance can be defined as the ability of the entire body or a part of the body to resist fatigue and to recover quickly after fatigue occurs. When you can maintain a given level of performance for longer periods of time, you are achieving a higher level of endurance.

The average physical education class meets for two or three one-hour periods per week. Most class time must be spent learning about the game and practicing skills and strategies. Therefore, the student who desires a higher level of conditioning than is possible through class participation must engage in additional activities outside of the classroom.

The only way to increase strength and endurance is by means of the *overload principle.* Overload for strength means that muscles must be "loaded" by increasing the resistance or stress beyond previous requirements. Overload for endurance means that the muscle group or the total body must be worked beyond previous repetition levels.

A detailed, technical discussion of muscular effectiveness cannot be presented here. Information concerning these matters can be found in current books and journals. A few conditioning exercises are briefly explained, however. These exercises can be performed in or out of class and will, for the most part, increase both strength and endurance.

General Exercises

1. Vigorous performance in sports and games.
2. Exercises in which the body weight is the resistance, for example, pullups, dips, rope climbing, and hanging-type activities.
3. Weight training equipment, including barbells, the Universal weight machine, and the Nautilus weight machine.
4. Isometric exercises in which there is muscular tension against a fixed object or another part of the body.
5. Interval training that involves a series of short periods (thirty to sixty seconds) of vigorous exercise with a short period (two or three minutes) of rest or light exercise between each work period.
6. Running on level ground and cross-country.
7. Calisthenics involving running in place, hopping, arm swinging, leg swinging, jumping, leg stretching, trunk rotation, trunk flexion, push-ups, sit-ups, leg lifts, and leg abduction and adduction.
8. Ball exercises that involve the skills and strategies of the game.

Using a heel kick, can you pass a stationary ball accurately to a teammate who is five yards behind you? Can you do the same after approaching the ball at a slow run? Can you direct the heel kick to a teammate who is following you as you dribble?

Specific Exercises

1. *Neck Flexion*   Lie on your back and bring your chin to your chest while someone applies a downward pressure at your forehead.
2. *Neck Extension and Hyperextension*   Lie face down and raise your head as far as possible while someone applies a downward pressure at the back of your head.
3. *Trunk Rotation*   Sit on the ground with your hands placed behind your head. Twist to one side as far as possible while someone applies a resisting pressure at your upper arms.
4. *Trunk Extension and Hyperextension*   Lie face down with your hands at the small of your back. Raise your head and trunk as far as possible while someone holds your feet down.
5. *Hip Flexion*   Sit on the edge of a table. Be sure that your leg is supported from the hip to the knee. Raise your thigh while someone applies a downward pressure at the knee.

6. *Hip Extension*   Rest the upper part of your body on a table with your face down. Hold the sides of the table and raise one leg with the knee straight while someone applies a downward pressure at the knee. Try this with pressure applied at the heel.
7. *Hip Adduction*   Lie on your back with your legs spread. Bring your legs together while someone applies outward pressure on the lower part of the legs.
8. *Hip Abduction*   Lie on your back with your legs together. Spread your legs apart while someone applies inward pressure on the lower part of the legs.
9. *Knee Extension*   Sit on the edge of a table. Be sure that your legs are supported from the hip to the knee. Raise your foot until your leg is fully extended while someone applies a downward pressure at the ankle.
10. *Knee Flexion*   Lie face down and flex your leg at the knee while someone applies a downward pressure at the ankle.

DETERMINING INSTRUCTIONAL GROUPS

Grouping students for instructional purposes is an important part of teaching physical activities. Generally, at the beginning of a soccer unit there is little time for elaborate skill-testing procedures. Most classes will have beginner, intermediate, and advanced skill levels. The instructor can utilize the time best and make the class more interesting and meaningful if students are grouped into these general categories for class instruction.

Possibly, the quickest way to place students in instructional groups is by means of a short, objective test. Ten to fifteen questions concerning soccer rules, skills, and strategies provide considerable information about students' backgrounds in soccer. This technique, coupled with a simple classification of skill by which students indicate their personal judgment about their skill and knowledge of soccer, is an effective means of establishing initial instructional groups. A classification scale such as the one included here can be used.

———— Beginner	Knows very little about soccer and has never received instruction or played the game.
———— Intermediate	Knows a little about soccer through previous instruction and class participation.
———— Advanced	Plays soccer on a regular basis and/or has played on competitive teams.

Skill-Test Items

If time permits, more elaborate skill-test items may be employed. Only brief descriptions of the skill test are included here. In each instance distribute the high ability players equally among the various teams or squads.

Obstacle Run   Time each class member as he or she runs an obstacle course. The obstacles may be chairs, wooden stands, hurdles (both high and low), side horses, and so on.

Kicking for Distance and/or Accuracy   Measure the distance each class member kicks the ball when using a specified soccer kick. If accuracy is the primary objective, allow each class member three specified kicks to another player or to a predetermined area.

Throwing for Distance and Accuracy   Measure the distance each class member can throw the ball by using a throw-in or any other type of throw used by the goalkeeper. If accuracy is the primary objective, allow each class member three specified throws to another player or to a predetermined area.

Sprinting   Time class members as they run the twenty-five, fifty, or seventy-five yard dash.

Standing Long Jump   Measure the distance each member can jump from a standing, two-foot takeoff.

Potato Race   Place two boxes fifteen yards apart with two tennis balls in the first box. The player reaches into the first box, secures one tennis ball, runs to the box fifteen yards away, and deposits the tennis ball into that box. The player then runs back to the first box, retrieves the second ball, returns to the second box to deposit it, and then finishes upon passing the first box.

BASIC SAFETY CONSIDERATIONS

One of the primary responsibilities of an instructor is the health and safety of class members. Each class period should be well organized, properly instructed, and adequately supervised during practice and game situations. Students, of course, must also assume their share of the responsibility for the health and safety of themselves and other class members. If the instructor and the students are aware of the potential hazards that can occur in a vigorous, running game such as soccer, many accidents and injuries can be avoided.

1. Select a field that is the appropriate size and is free from obstructions on or holes in the area of play.
2. Provide proper class organization, instruction, and supervision.
3. Provide proper conditioning of class members prior to vigorous activity.
4. Allow time for warming up during the first few minutes of each class.
5. Stress the proper execution of skills and a basic knowledge of game rules.
6. Provide adequate officiating in game situations.
7. Do not allow horseplay of any kind in class.
8. During game situations watch for undue fatigue.
9. Avoid fast-moving drills and games on rainy days.
10. Make provisions for the treatment of minor cuts, bruises, and blisters.

patterns of play

7

The purpose of this chapter is to enable each student to—

1. identify the positions and responsibilities of each player on a soccer team,
2. be aware of various defensive and offensive systems used in playing the game,
3. differentiate between the long-passing and short-passing attacks,
4. cite examples of principles that show a basic understanding of offensive and defensive strategies,
5. recognize that set plays are an important part of offensive strategy.

For a team to be effective, all players must assume responsibility for their individual positions. Moreover, players must be aware of the positions and responsibilities of their teammates.

THE TWO-BACK SYSTEM

The following discussion concerning players and their positions is based on the 2-3-5 system or the two-back game. Although this system is old, it is quite effective with beginners. Since beginners in soccer lack advanced skills and maneuvers and have not yet learned intricate offenses, they are able to play and enjoy the two-back game without taking undue advantage of only two defensive players.

After players become proficient in skills and maneuvers and gain the necessary understanding of soccer, they should be introduced to the three- or four-back game. Brief discussions of these systems are presented later in the chapter.

Why is it important for the goalkeeper to advance as a potential scorer approaches?

Fig. 7.1   Area of play for goalkeeper

The Goalkeeper

The goalkeeper should be physically agile and mentally alert. Generally, a skilled basketball player who has good height and reach possesses the necessary qualifications.

The goalkeeper constitutes the last stage of defense and the first stage of offense. Thus, your job as goalie is not only to keep the opponent from scoring, but also to clear the ball from the goal area. Your primary position of play is within the penalty area (fig. 7.1). You should assume a well balanced stance, two or three paces in front of the goal line, facing the ball. When attempting to pick up a potential scorer, you should advance to reduce the angle of the shot, being careful not to let the scorer get inside the goal area with the ball. It is evident, then, that a considerable amount of play by the goalkeeper will occur outside the goal area, but within the penalty area. Although the goalkeeper may play the ball outside the penalty area, the ball may not be touched with the hands outside this area. Common sense and good goaltending suggest that the goalie remain within the penalty area when possible.

If you are an inexperienced goalkeeper, you should be extremely careful about leaving the goal unguarded when you do not have the ball. In general, you should leave the net only in a desperation charge at a dribbler or in an attempt to get to the ball before anyone else does.

The goalkeeper's position of play affords the best opportunity of directing the defense, especially the fullbacks and halfbacks. Cooperative efforts between the goalkeeper and the backs will develop better individual play and will improve defensive strategy.

The Fullbacks

The right and left fullbacks are basically defensive players. They must have the ability to size up situations correctly and quickly; they must be alert and aggressive. Your primary position of play as fullback is approximately a quarter section of your half of the field (fig. 7.2). Each fullback, however, in many game situations will extend the area of play to include the entire penalty area to the middle of the field. The fullbacks should seldom, if ever, cross the half-way line and leave the goal area unprotected.

Fig. 7.2   Area of play for left fullback

When the right fullback moves toward the right to tackle the opposing out-side left, what should the left fullback do?

The two fullbacks should be in staggered positions at all times. You mark the outside forward on your side of the field. When you move out to play the ball or tackle an opponent, your counterpart must move to the middle of the field to afford adequate cover. The two fullbacks must not only work together, but must also be alert to directions from the goalkeeper. Above all, they must not crowd the goalkeeper or interfere with the goalkeeper's play. One of the fullbacks should be ready to move into the goal area if the goalkeeper is forced to leave the goal unprotected. It must be remembered, however, that the full-backs cannot touch the ball with their hands.

Fullbacks should possess the ability to kick the ball with either foot. The major objective of the fullbacks is to clear the ball to a teammate if possible. The accomplishment of this objective may necessitate kicking the ball to the goal-keeper or to any other teammate who is not being closely marked. It may mean kicking the ball out-of-bounds under a pressed attack. The two most useful kicks for fullbacks are the volley and half-volley. Two particularly dangerous situations that fullbacks should avoid are dribbling and passing in front of the goal. Obviously, these tactics should be employed only when there is adequate space and time, conditions seldom enjoyed by fullbacks.

The Halfbacks

The center half and the right and left halfbacks form the backbone of the soc-cer team. As key players they must be fast, energetic, and in especially good physical condition. They also must possess skill in kicking, heading, and tack-ling. Each of these positions requires alert defensive and offensive play.

The position of play for the center half is the middle of the field, between the right and left halfbacks. As center half you are responsible for that portion of the field extending from your own goal area to the opponent's penalty area

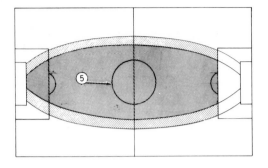

Fig. 7.3   Area of play for center halfback

(fig. 7.3). On defense you mark the opposing center forward and attempt to stop any down-the-middle attack. On offense you attempt to pass the ball ahead to your own forwards.

The central position of the center half affords you the opportunity to direct the attack. Although you will attempt to score occasionally, you should lob the ball into the penalty area so others can try for a goal in most instances.

The position of play for the halfbacks can be understood best by looking at figure 7.4. As halfback you should seldom advance more than three-fourths of the length of the field. In other words, you must avoid going too far up field in the attack and, thereby, neglect defensive duties.

Defensively, halfbacks usually mark the inside forward on their side of the field. There will be times, however, when it will be necessary for you to mark the outside forward or the center forward. In all cases you should force the dribbler to the outside of the field.

Offensively, the halfback provides support for the forward line. Your ability to pass the ball accurately sets the stage for the attack. Since you are usually responsible for throw-ins, you should develop the ability to throw the ball accurately.

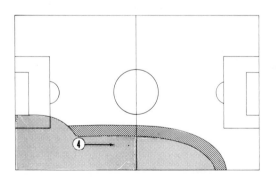

Fig. 7.4   Area of play for right halfback

The Forwards

The center forward, the inside right, the inside left, the outside right, and the outside left form the forward line of a soccer team. Since these players carry the attack deep into the opponent's territory, they have many opportunities to score goals. In order that they can carry out their assignments effectively, both offensively and defensively, they must possess skill, stamina, speed, and general fitness.

Ideally, as center forward you should be above average in size, skill, and speed. Your size should permit you to charge and tackle heavier opponents. You should be well versed in heading, kicking, turning, and passing with either foot. You should have the ability to move about quickly so that you can receive passes, execute passes, mark the opposing center half, or harass the opposing backs as the situation may warrant.

Can you match each halfback with the attacking player he normally marks?

The center forward is first and foremost, however, an offensive player. You are often referred to as an "opportunist". Although you will shoot many times and score many goals, it is important for you to look for opportunities to pass to the inside forwards or outside forwards when you are closely marked. By playing a waiting game, you provide an excellent decoy and are fresh when the attack gets underway. Your position of play is the middle of the field in an area from the center circle to the opponent's goal area (fig. 7.5).

The right and left inside forwards do not require the speed of outside forwards, but they must have the ability to work tirelessly. Offensively, the inside forward acts in the capacity of a playmaker. You may be able to draw the opponent out of position by means of a dribble or work the ball to a teammate who is not closely marked by means of an accurate pass. The tactic of passing the ball to the inside forward and then switching positions will help to confuse the opponent. Frequently, a long, accurate pass to the far outside forward will set up a scoring situation on the weak side. A valuable maneuver for one of the in-

Fig. 7.5   Area of play for center forward

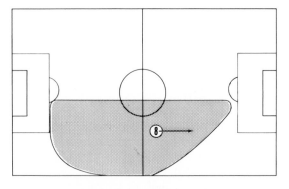

Fig. 7.6   Area of play for inside right

side forwards is that of following up attempted goal shots in an effort to get a second try for a goal.

The position of play for the inside forwards can be readily observed in figure 7.6. As indicated, the inside forwards narrow their area of play as they approach the penalty area. It should be noted that these players must avoid going too far upfield in the attack, for if they do they will necessarily neglect their defensive duties.

Defensively, you must mark the opposing halfback, assist your own halfbacks in stopping offensive moves down the field, and cover the opposing inside forward on throw-ins taken by the opponents.

The outside forward positions call for players who have speed and skill in passing, dribbling, and ball control. Insofar as speed is concerned, the outside forwards must be able to stay with or ahead of the ball at all times. Also, they must be able to outmaneuver their opponents if they are to be effective during the attack.

To play the outside forward position, you must have the ability to kick long, accurate passes at the proper time. Even though you shoot on occasions and sometimes score many goals, you should constantly watch for opportunities to center the ball to the center forward or cross the ball to the opposite inside forward or outside forward. In addition to long passes, you will execute many short passes in your cooperative efforts with the inside forwards and halfbacks.

When playing the outside forward position, the touchline on one side of you and the opponent on the opposite side limit your area of play. Under these conditions, dribbling can be used to an advantage. A well executed dribble can be used to draw the opponent out of position or from in front of the goal before passing to a teammate. The ability to receive passes on the run from any direction and to maintain control of the ball will enable you to dribble, pass, or shoot to a distinct advantage.

The position of play for the outside forwards is shown in figure 7.7. Normally, the outside forward plays six or seven yards in from the touchline; however, you must be ready to move toward the goal area when the situation warrants it. Generally, you will kick all corner kicks. Game conditions will govern placement of the corner kick. On throw-ins by the opponent, you should cover the opposing fullback.

Fig. 7.7   Area of play for outside left

THE THREE-BACK SYSTEM

It might be wise to point out that limited class time, large class enrollments, and even limited facilities and equipment may not permit a thorough coverage of all the systems of the game of soccer. Be that as it may, the third-player back game is quite popular in competitive soccer and could be taught to intermediate or advanced soccer players.

When the center halfback plays as the third back between the two full-backs, one of the major responsibilities of that position is defense. The main job is to cover the middle area in front of the goal and stop the down-the-middle attack. The center half then, in the role of defender, should seldom, if ever, cross the halfway line.

The loss of the center halfback on offense will, of necessity, increase the area to be covered by the right and left halfbacks. They must widen and extend their area of play to approximately the entire length and one-half the width of the field so that there is adequate coverage.

Similarly, the area of play for the forwards will change somewhat. The inside forwards should cover approximately one-half the field from their own penalty area to the opposing goal box. The outside forwards should come back farther and widen their area of play so that they cover approximately three-fourths the length and one-half the width of the field.

This system has the advantage of having three backs on defense. It is an effective defense against the W offense; however, it is ineffective in the face of a four-player attacking offense. Moreover, it creates troublesome spaces in the defensive half of the field.

THE FOUR-BACK SYSTEM

The four-back system is a more intricate development in defensive strategy. It was devised to lessen the effectiveness of the four-player attacking offense. It is a difficult defensive system to employ successfully, and it requires highly skilled players who are well versed in all aspects of the game.

The four-back game retains the center halfback as the third back and calls upon one of the wing halfbacks to play as the fourth fullback. It then becomes necessary for one of the forwards to play the halfback position. The alignment of players under these conditions becomes 4-2-4.

The four fullbacks have the primary responsibility of defense. The two outside backs mark the opposing wings, and the two center backs stop the down-the-middle attack. The fullbacks, in their roles as defenders, should not cross the halfway line.

Of the three defensive systems described in the text, which places the heaviest demands on the forwards? Which is effective against the W offense? Which is intended to combat a four-man offense?

The area of play for the halfbacks and forwards remains much the same as in the three-back game. The two halfbacks provide support for the forward line on offense and assist the fullbacks on defense when they are needed.

There are, of course, other defensive systems used by competitive soccer teams. However, most of these systems are too intricate for beginners and require players with considerable ability and knowledge of the game. Therefore, they will not be discussed here. Information concerning these systems can be found in current soccer coaching books and periodicals.

DEVELOPING THE OFFENSE

The two main types of offense are the long-passing and the short-passing attacks. The long-passing attack yields large yardage gains, the element of surprise, and many scoring opportunities, but it reduces control of the ball and cannot be used successfully against a strong wind. The short-passing attack gives better ball control and decreases opportunities for interception, but it requires very accurate passing and good ground conditions. Since each type of attack has its advantages and disadvantages, the type employed should be chosen according to the ability of the players, game situations, and weather conditions.

A and B (team 1) are attempting to move the ball toward their opponent's goal in the direction of the arrow. As Y (team 2) approaches, A passes the ball to B. What mistakes have A and B made?

Basic Formations

These formations afford starting points for the attack. The formations should not be viewed as inflexible or unchangeable, since the manner in which the attack finally is carried out depends upon the players and game situations.

The W formation (fig. 7.8), the M formation (fig. 7.9), and the spearhead formation (fig. 7.10) are based on the following principles:

1. Pass the ball to the attack areas or to open spaces near players. For example, in the W formation the inside forwards pass the ball to the attack areas in front of the center or outside forwards.
2. Attack in depth, or in waves of players. Players should avoid forming a straight line across the field as they approach the penalty area.
3. Practice interchanging positions in an effort to confuse the defense.
4. Carry the attack on a wide front in order to spread out the defense.
5. Use forward and backward passes to keep your opponent off guard.
6. Switch the play from one side of the field to the other by kicking the ball back and forth across the field.
7. Use elements of surprise and suddenness to outmaneuver your opponent.
8. Notice positions of players so that you can utilize open spaces as the attack unfolds.
9. Set up plays in advance and attempt to carry them out even though teammates may be closely guarded.

Fig. 7.8   W formation

Fig. 7.9   M formation

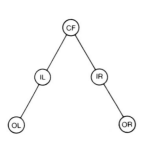

Fig. 7.10   Spearhead formation

Set Plays   Kickoff plays, throw-in plays, corner kicks, and goal kicks are important parts of offensive strategy. Through predetermined and well-practiced sets plays, your team will be able to retain possession of the ball and make progress in advancing toward the opponent's goal.

Kickoff plays are numerous and varied. In order to vary your offense and deceive the opponents, plays should be devised that involve the forwards, the center half, or the halfbacks. An example of a play involving the center half follows:

1. The center forward kicks off to the inside right forward and runs downfield ready to receive a pass.
2. The other forwards also run downfield ready to receive a pass.
3. The inside right forward passes back to the center half, who, in turn, makes a long downfield kick to one of the forwards.

Assuming that the players are good passers and that the ground is in good condition but the wind is strong, which type of passing attack would you recommend and why?

Throw-in plays are important because of the scoring opportunities that can occur as a result of them. The type of throw-in play to be used will be governed by the position of the ball and the tactics of the defense. Other suggestions regarding throw-in plays follow.

1. In general, throw the ball to the feet of all teammates except to the goalkeeper, who should receive the ball chest-high.
2. When in the defensive end of the field, throw the ball away from the goal area, unless throwing directly to the goalkeeper.
3. When near midfield, a throw-in play involving any of a number of players is possible. Don't follow the same procedure all the time.
4. When in the offensive end of the field, a throw-in to any temporarily unmarked player may put the ball into scoring position.

When the goal kick is taken from your own goal, the goalkeeper generally kicks the ball. Duties of the other players then may be as follows:

1. One fullback guards the goal while the goalkeeper kicks.
2. The other fullback marks the opposing center forward.
3. The halfbacks mark the opposing inside forwards.
4. The ball is kicked to either side of midfield, and the forwards set up the attack.

Additional goal kick plays involving other players are possible. In any event, don't follow the same procedure all the time.

The corner kick provides an excellent opportunity for scoring since a goal may be made directly from it. Important points to bear in mind when this situation arises are:

1. Take the corner kick quickly before the defenders can set up a solid defense.
2. The kicker, usually the outside forward, should vary the kick in both height and spin.
3. Position the forwards to work as a unit when receiving the ball, or move them back to the penalty area line to draw out the defenders.

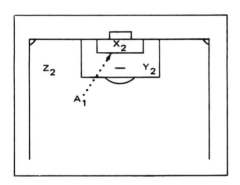

A_1 (attacking team) shoots the ball at the goal. X_2 (defending team) catches the ball. What should X do now? What should Y_2, Z_2, and A_1 do?

DEVELOPING THE DEFENSE

The two main types of defense are the zone and the player-for-player. In the zone defense you are responsible for guarding the offensive player with the ball when that player is in your zone or area. This type of defense is recommended for beginning players since it stresses positional play. Its major weakness lies in the fact that it does not provide cover for every player in the attack.

The player-for-player defense requires that each player guard a particular opponent throughout defensive situations no matter where that player is. Although this type of defense provides adequate cover for all attackers, it also requires skilled players. If you are outmaneuvered by your opponent, it is necessary for one of your teammates to come to your aid.

In order to gain the advantages of each type of defense, a combination zone and player-for-player defense can be employed. The players in the immediate area of the ball mark the attackers in that area. When the ball moves to another area, the players closest to it mark the attackers. Within striking distance of the goal, every player is marked closely.

Basic principles to bear in mind when developing defensive strategy are:

1. Arrange the defense in depth or in waves of players. Avoid forming a straight line of players when nearing your own goal area.
2. Keep your defense in close; the more spread out the defense, the more vulnerable it is.

3. When a teammate tackles the player with the ball, mark the player who is left unguarded. Avoid two-on-one or three-on-two situations.
4. Be ready to provide assistance or to back up play in the area where the ball is located.
5. Retreat slowly when necessary in order to enable your teammates to set up the defense.
6. Pass the ball to the goalkeeper when pressed by the attackers so that the ball may be cleared from the goal area.
7. Defensive halfbacks should converge toward the goal as play draws near the goal area.

Soccer, like most games, is largely a matter of using your wits, but before you can outmaneuver your opponent you have to have the skill and knowledge to do so. In addition, the eleven players comprising the soccer team must be able to blend their skills and knowledge so that they perform as an efficient unit rather than as an aimless group of individuals.

rules of the game
8

The purpose of this chapter is to enable each student to—

1. examine the most important rules of soccer,
2. synthesize information pertaining to each of the rules of the game,
3. accurately interpret game rules in order to improve skill in and enjoyment of the game.

A summary of the most important rules of soccer is presented in the following pages. Most rules are the same for men and women. Differences for women are listed at the end of the chapter. Those students who desire a more detailed analysis of the rules should refer to the NCAA Soccer Guide[1] and the NAGWS Soccer Guide.[2] Substantial portions of the rules may change from year to year. For an up-to-date interpretation of the rules, the current editions of the rule guides should be consulted.

START OF PLAY

The game is started from the center spot within the center circle by means of a place kick into the opponent's half of the field of play. The following stipulations govern the kickoff:

1. Before the ball is kicked, all players must be in their own half of the field.
2. Players of the opposing team must be outside the center circle (ten yards away) until the ball travels *forward* at least the distance of its circumference, i.e., twenty-seven inches.
3. A goal cannot be scored directly from a kickoff.
4. The player who kicks the ball cannot play it a second time until it has been played or touched by another player.
5. The ball can be kicked in any direction by any player after a proper kickoff.

1. Adapted from the *1979 NCAA Soccer 39th Annual Guide*, National Collegiate Athletic Association (Shawnee Mission, Kansas).
2. Adapted from the *1979 NAGWS Guide, Soccer*, American Alliance for Health, Physical Education, and Recreation (Washington, D.C.).

Penalty for Improper Kickoff

1. The kickoff is retaken for an infringement of stipulations 1, 2, or 3.
2. An indirect free kick is awarded to the opposing team for an infringement of stipulation 4.

After a goal is scored, the ball is kicked off by the team against which the goal was scored. At the start of the second half, teams change ends of the field, and the team that kicked off at the start of the previous period receives the kickoff.

The ball is put into play by means of a drop ball for any other temporary suspension of play, except in the case of a free kick or a throw-in. The drop occurs at the point where the ball was when play was suspended, and players cannot touch the ball until it touches the ground. If play is suspended when the ball is in the penalty area, the ball is dropped at the nearest point outside the penalty area.

The markings on the soccer field are considered in play. The ball is therefore in play until it completely crosses the goal or touchlines either in the air or on the ground. In addition, the ball is in play if it returns to the field of play after striking a goalpost, crossbar, or corner flag. It is also in play if it touches either referee in the field of play.

In all cases, it is the position of the ball that is important. For example, a ball in the air that passes out of play and returns to the field of play should be given out of play, or as long as the ball remains inside the field of play, a player outside the playing area may play the ball.

In order to score a goal, the ball must completely cross the goal line, between the goalposts, and under the crossbar. The attacking team cannot score a goal by using the hands or arms.

OFFSIDE

The offside rule prevents a player from interfering with an opponent or with the play. It also prevents a player from remaining close to the goal area where a goal could be scored from short range. If you are nearer to the opponent's goal line than the ball when the ball is played, you are offside unless:

1. You are in your own half of the field of play.
2. There are two opponents nearer to their goal line than you.
3. The ball was last touched or played by an opponent.
4. You receive the ball directly from a goal kick, corner kick, throw-in, or drop by the referee.

Penalty for Infraction of Offside Rule

1. An indirect free kick is taken by a player of the opposing team.
2. Unless interfering with play or seeking to gain an advantage, an offside player is not penalized.

VIOLATIONS

Penalties are imposed upon players who commit intentional fouls or are involved in misconduct such as:

1. Kicking, striking, or jumping at an opponent.
2. Tripping or stooping in front of or behind an opponent.
3. Handling the ball (other than the goalkeeper within the penalty area).
4. Holding, pushing, obstructing with the hand or arm, or using the knee against an opponent.
5. Charging an opponent in a violent or dangerous manner.
6. Charging the goalkeeper when he or she is in possession of the ball.
7. Kicking the ball when it is in the possession of the goalkeeper.
8. Obstructing an opponent, i.e., running between an opponent and the ball or using the body as an obstacle to block the path of an opponent.
9. Engaging in dangerous play, i.e., play that is likely to cause injury.

When would it be legal to charge the goalkeeper?

AWARDED KICKS AND THE THROW-IN

Free kicks are classified as direct, from which a goal can be scored directly, and indirect, from which a goal cannot be scored until the ball has been touched by another player. Direct free kicks are awarded for major infractions of the rules and for personal misconduct. (Direct kicks awarded to the offensive team in the penalty area are penalty kicks; a free kick awarded to the defensive team in the penalty area must be kicked out of the penalty area.) Offenses for which a direct free kick is given include:

1. Offenses committed with the hands or arms (handling the ball, holding, using hands or arms on an opponent in order to reach the ball, pushing, and striking).
2. Offenses committed with the feet and legs (kicking, tripping, use of the knee, and jumping at an opponent).
3. Offenses concerned with charging violently or dangerously (failure of both players to be in an upright position, to be within playing distance of the ball, to have at least one foot on the ground, or to hold the arms close to the body).
4. Offenses involving the goalkeeper (handling by the goalkeeper outside the penalty area, handling by a new goalkeeper who has failed to properly notify the referee, charging the goalkeeper in the penalty area, and intentionally throwing or striking an opponent with the ball by the goalkeeper).

Indirect free kicks are awarded for minor infractions of the rules and for technical violations. Offenses for which an indirect free kick is given include:

1. Offenses concerned with a player kicking the ball a second time before it is played by another player (kickoffs, throw-in, free kick, corner kick, and goal kick if the ball has passed outside the penalty area).
2. Offenses committed during the penalty kick (ball not kicked forward).
3. Offenses involving the goalkeeper (carrying the ball by the goalkeeper more than four steps without bouncing it, and delaying the game by not getting rid of the ball).
4. Offenses involving persons on the sidelines (substitution made at improper time, substitute failing to report to the referee, illegal coaching from sidelines after a warning).
5. Offenses concerned with unsportsmanlike conduct (arguing with the referee, ungentlemanly or unladylike conduct, dangerous play, and failure to leave the field of play after ordered to do so).
6. Offenses concerned with offside.
7. Offenses concerned with improper charging, interfering with goalkeeper, obstruction other than holding.

When a free kick is being taken, all members of the opposing team must remain ten yards away from the ball until it is in play, i.e., until it has traveled the distance of its circumference.

A *penalty kick* is awarded to the offended team for *deliberate* fouls committed by the defensive team in its own penalty area. Infringements of the rules must be those that are penalized by a direct free kick. The kick is taken from the penalty mark. The following stipulations govern the penalty kick:

1. Only the player taking the kick and the opposing goalkeeper may play the ball.
2. All other players must be outside the penalty area, at least ten yards from the penalty mark but within the field of play.
3. Without moving the feet, the goalkeeper must stand on the goal line until the ball is kicked.
4. The player must kick the ball forward and cannot play the ball a second time until it has been touched by another player.

Penalty for Improper Penalty Kick

1. The kick is retaken for an infringement of the foregoing stipulations by the defending team if a goal has not resulted.
2. The kick is retaken for an infringement by any member of the attacking team other than the player kicking the ball if a goal is scored.
3. An indirect free kick is awarded to the opposing team for an infringement by the player kicking the ball.

A_1 (attacking team) shoots the ball at the goal. X_2 (defending team) catches the ball and plays it so that B_1 gains possession. B_1 shoots and scores a goal. Is A_1 or B_1 offside?

A *throw-in* from the touchline is awarded when the ball passes completely over a touchline either on the ground or in the air. The ball is thrown in from the spot where it crossed the touchline. The following stipulations govern the throw-in:

1. The throw-in is taken by a player of the team opposite to that of the player who last touched the ball.
2. The thrower must face the field of play and must have part of each foot either on the touchline or on the ground outside the touchline at the moment the ball is delivered.
3. The thrower must use both hands equally and must deliver the ball from behind and overhead.
4. The ball may be thrown in any direction.
5. The thrower may not play the ball a second time until it has been touched by another player.
6. A goal cannot be scored directly from a throw-in.

Penalty for improper throw-in:

1. The throw-in is taken by a player of the opposing team for an infringement of stipulations 2 or 3.
2. An indirect free kick is awarded to the opposing team for an infringement of stipulation 5.

A *goal kick* is awarded when the ball is last touched by an offensive player and passes over the goal line without resulting in a goal. The kick is made by a defender from a point within that half of the goal area nearest to where the ball crossed the line. The following stipulations govern the goal kick:

1. The ball must be kicked from the ground in any direction beyond the penalty area.
2. The kicker cannot play the ball a second time until it has been touched by another player.
3. A goal cannot be scored directly from a goal kick since it is an indirect free kick.

Penalty for Improper Goal Kick

1. The kick is retaken if the ball is not kicked beyond the penalty area.
2. An indirect free kick is awarded to the opposing team for an infringement by the player who is kicking.

A *corner kick* is awarded when the ball is last touched by a defensive player and passes over the goal line without resulting in a goal. The kick is made by a member of the attacking team from within the quarter-circle at the nearest corner flag post. The following stipulations govern the corner kick:

1. A goal may be scored directly from such a kick.
2. Members of the opposing team must remain ten yards away from the ball until it travels the distance of its circumference.
3. The kicker cannot play the ball a second time until it has been touched by another player.

Penalty for Improper Corner Kick

1. The kick is retaken for an infringement of stipulation 2.
2. An indirect free kick is awarded to the opposing team for an infringement of stipulation 3.

RULE DIFFERENCES FOR WOMEN

1. Every player must wear shin guards for protection of the legs.
2. A goal kick is awarded when a goal is scored directly from a kickoff.
3. A direct free kick is awarded for *attempting* to trip, kick, strike, or jump at an opponent.
4. A direct free kick is awarded for executing a sliding tackle (considered an attempt to trip an opponent).
5. Protection of the chest is not considered handling the ball. The forearms must be in contact with the body and the palms of the hands must be flat against the body.
6. An indirect free kick is awarded for playing the ball while sitting or lying on the ground if the player is within six feet of an opponent.

unwritten rules

9

The purpose of this chapter is to enable each student to—

1. examine, interpret, and apply unwritten rules in relation to game situations.

Courtesy and sportsmanship are as much a part of sports activities as are the skills and rules of the game. No one enjoys playing a game with a person who is a "hothead" or a "complainer," and no doubt those individuals who cannot control their emotions do not really enjoy the game. This certainly does not mean that you must give up aggressive play or the will to win; however, it does mean that each player has the responsibility of developing emotional control. Learning to accept situations as they occur and developing respect for your teammates, your opponents, and the officials are major steps in this direction. Remember that courtesy and sportsmanship cannot be imposed on players by means of rules. These concepts emerge only as individual players gain understanding of and respect for the spirit of rules. The following list of game courtesies should help you develop better sportsmanship and increase your enjoyment of soccer.

1. Always play your best and play to win, but play for fun.
2. When you are aware that you have committed an infringement of the rules, notify the official by raising your hand over your head. For example, if you touched the ball last before it went out-of-bounds, or if you touched the ball with your hand or arm, raise your hand.
3. Leave your temper and inappropriate language in the locker room. Derogatory remarks will not improve your game.
4. Keep the game moving. Move the required distance from the ball for free kicks as quickly as possible. Be ready to start play immediately upon the referee's signal.
5. Don't criticize the play of others, and don't blame others for your own poor playing.
6. Be humble in victory and gracious in defeat.
7. Congratulate your opponent, and extend thanks to the officials after the game, whether you win or lose.

facts for enthusiasts
10

The purpose of this chapter is to enable each student to—

1. conclude that very little personal soccer equipment is needed to play the game,
2. cite examples to show the importance of selection and care of equipment,
3. recognize that there are many soccer enthusiasts throughout the world.

FACTS ABOUT EQUIPMENT

Unless you become a member of an organized soccer team or club, you will find that very little personal equipment is needed to enjoy the game. For most school or recreational purposes, all that actually is needed is a soccer ball and wearing apparel appropriate to vigorous activity. Even then, the soccer ball does not have to meet official specifications.

As members of a team or club, players wear jerseys, shorts, a special soccer shoe, shin guards, and long stockings. The soccer shoe is the most important part of the player's equipment. A regulation shoe is high-laced and cleated with aluminum, leather, rubber, nylon, or steel tipped plastic to prevent slipping. The shoe must conform to specifications related to the width and length of cleats.

The official soccer ball must meet several specifications concerned with inflation, circumference, and weight. The leather covered soccer ball must be 27 to 28 inches in circumference and 14 to 16 ounces in weight at the start of the game. It cannot exceed 16.75 ounces even when wet and used. The inflation pressure of the ball is not stated in pounds but rather is indicated by stating the number of inches (100) from which it must be dropped to a smooth cement surface and the number of inches (60 to 65) to which it must rebound.

When selecting equipment such as shoes or a ball, you should keep several points in mind. The shoes should be of a good grade of leather and should fit comfortably. Proper drying of shoes after use and proper storage of shoes when not in use are important aspects of their care.

Whether you select a rubber-covered ball or a leather-covered ball is a matter of personal preference. The rubber-covered ball is an all-purpose ball and requires little care. The leather-covered ball should be cleaned periodically with saddle soap or a similar cleaner. If the ball becomes wet, it should be placed in a warm room to dry. Both the rubber- and leather-covered balls should be partially deflated and stored in a dry place when not in use.

FACTS ABOUT CURRENT PLAY

The Intercollegiate Soccer Football Association and the National Collegiate Athletic Association have sponsored the NCAA tournament since 1959. The St. Louis University Billikens dominated intercollegiate soccer until recent years. A victory in 1973 gave the Billikens their tenth National Collegiate Championship in fifteen years. Although the St. Louis area still produces nationally ranked teams, regional and tournament play has brought forth a host of new soccer powers. The San Francisco Dons made a bid to win their third straight national championship in 1977, but were defeated by Hartwick College. However, the Dons defeated Indiana easily in 1978 to post their third title in four years. Other teams that have won the NCAA tournament include the United States Naval Academy, Michigan State University, the University of Maryland, and Howard University.

There are many international "heroes" or outstanding players of the game. Edson Arantes Do Nascimento, or as he is known in the soccer world, Pelé, is probably the world's finest soccer player. His accomplishment of scoring the one thousandth goal of his professional career has made him the top goal scorer in professional and modern soccer. In 1974, Pelé announced his retirement from soccer. The New York Cosmos, however, were able to lure the thirty-four-year-old star back to the game. He made his debut for the Cosmos in June, 1975, and retired at the conclusion of the 1977 season.

references and resources

BAILY, R. "Player-For-Player Defense," *Athletic Journal*, 58 (May, 1978), 60.

———. "Blizzards of Joy Down in Argentina," *Sports Illustrated*, 50 (February, 1979), 106.

BYRNE, E. C. "He Who Controls the Midfield," *Scholastic Coach*, 48 (October, 1978), 40.

CHYZOWYCH, WALTER. *The Official Soccer Book of the United States Soccer Federation*. Chicago: Rand McNally, 1978.

DAVIS, W. W. and S. B. SNOW. "Funnel Tactical Team Defense," *Scholastic Coach*, 48 (February, 1979), 32.

GAMMON, C. "Total Soccer Could Be a Dutch Treat," *Sports Illustrated*, 50 April, 1979), 71.

GAMMON, C. "Two in a Row for the Cosmos; Soccer Bowl Victory Over Tampa Bay Rowdies," *Sports Illustrated*, 49 (September, 1978), 18.

HESS, R. F. "Thinking a Head," *Scholastic Coach*, 47 (August, 1977), 64.

HIRSHEY, D. "Taken on the Grand Tour; Cosmos vs. European Teams," *Sports Illustrated*, 49 (October, 1978), 110.

KEETON, GEORGE W. *The Football Revolution*. Newton Abbot: David and Charles Publishers, 1972.

LEBOW, JARED. *All About Soccer*. New York: Newsweeks Books, 1978.

MAHER, A. E. "Basic Soccer Passing," *Scholastic Coach*, 47 (September, 1977), 55.

MAHER, A. E. "Developing Numerical Superiority Near the Ball," *Scholastic Coach*, 41 (August, 1979), 44.

MAISNER, LARRY. *Practical Soccer Tactics for Youth Coaches*. Mountain View, Ca.: World Publications, 1979.

MASLOW, J. E. "Can the U. S. Play Soccer with the Big Boys?" *Saturday Review*, 5 (October, 1978), 49.

McKECHNEY, R. "Offensive Throw In," *Athletic Journal*, 59 (September, 1978), 32.

MENKE, FRANK G. *The Encyclopedia of Sports*. South Brunswick, N.J.: A. S. Barnes and Company, 1975.

National Association for Girls and Women in Sport. *NAGWS Guide, Soccer*. Washington, D.C.: American Alliance for Health, Physical Education, and Recreation, 1979.

National Collegiate Athletic Association. *The 1979 Soccer, 39th Annual Guide.* Shawnee Mission, Kansas: National Collegiate Athletic Association, 1979.

REED, J. D. "Coming of Age in Seattle; U. S. Olympic and National Teams," *Sports Illustrated,* 50 (February, 1979), 42.

REED, J. D. "Hot Foot for the Hoosiers; Indiana vs. St. Louis University," *Sports Illustrated,* 49 (October, 1979), 94.

REED, J. D. "Not Settling for Hamburger; North American Soccer League's 13th Season," *Sports Illustrated,* 50 (March, 1979), 38.

REED, J. D. "They Flunked Foreign Affairs; San Francisco vs. Indiana in NCAA Soccer Finals," *Sports Illustrated,* 49 (December, 1978), 18.

REID, A. "Argentina! World Cup," *New Yorker,* 54 (August, 1978), 37.

REIN, R. K. "Peripatetic Pele Leaves Home Without It," *People,* 10 (July, 1978), 30.

SABIE, MOHAMEND. *Soccer for Teaching and Coaching.* Champaign, Ill.: Stipes Publishing Company, 1976.

SOAR, PHIL. *Soccer: The World Game.* New York: St. Martin's Press, 1978.

VAN WIEREN, G. "Cardiovascular Endurance in Soccer Players," *Athletic Journal,* 59 (September, 1978), 74.

VOGELSINGER, HUBERT. *The Challenge of Soccer.* Boston: Allyn and Bacon, 1973.

List of Resources

The New York Times Index.

Soccer America, P. O. Box 23704, Oakland, California 94623. (Published weekly.) Printed by B & B Printing, Albany. Business Address: 1519 Shattuck Avenue, Berkeley, California 94709.

Soccer Corner, Daisy-Hi Torque Publishing Company, 16200 Ventura Boulevard, Encino, California 91436. (Published 8/year.)

Soccer Digest, Century Publishing Company, 1020 Church Street, Evanston, Illinois 60201. (Published 6/year.)

Soccer Journal, National Soccer Coaches Association of America, 668 La Vista Creek, Walnut Creek, California 94598. (Published quarterly.)

Soccer News, Soccer Associates, Inc., Box 634, New Rochelle, New York 10802. (Published monthly.)

Soccer World, World Publications, Box 366, Mountain View, California 94040. (Published weekly.)

Audio-Visual Materials

Soccer. Individual cartridges in color, stressing basic and advanced skills, team play, game strategies. Champions on Film, 745 State Circle, Ann Arbor, Michigan 48104.

Soccer. Match films, NASL Series Training Films and King Football Series Training Films. Modern Film Rentals, 2323 New Hyde Park Road, New Hyde Park, New York 11040 (requires NSCAA membership).

Soccer: Do's and Don'ts of Passing. Analyzes the passing game and discusses factors that lead to efficient and inefficient teamwork (25 minutes; b & w; 1972). University of Iowa, AV Center, C-5 East Hall, Iowa City, Iowa 52242.

Soccer: Dribbling and Feinting. Emphasizes beginning through advanced maneuvers and drills (15 minutes; color; 1974). Brigham Young University, Educational Media Center, 290 Herold R. Clark Building, Provo, Utah 84602.

Soccer Exercises and Tactics for Everyone. Stresses warm-up exercises and lead-up games to develop conditioning, skills, and team play (20 minutes; color; 1976). University of Wisconsin/Madison, Bureau of Audio-Visual Instruction, 1327 University Avenue, Madison, Wisconsin 53706.

Soccer Fundamentals for Everyone. Emphasizes basic knowledge and skills, practice formations and game situations (12 minutes; color; 1976). University of Wisconsin/Madison, Bureau of Audio-Visual Instruction, 1327 University Avenue, Madison, Wisconsin 53706.

Soccer: Hands Off. Introduces game play and explains basic skills. A film for young people of all ages (16 minutes; color; 1975). Indiana University, Audio Visual Center, Bloomington, Indiana 47401.

Soccer: Head to Toe. Introduces basic skills and rules of the game (14 minutes; color; 1975). University of Wisconsin/Madison, Bureau of Audio-Visual Instruction, 1327 University Avenue, Madison, Wisconsin 53706.

Soccer: Juggling and Trapping. Demonstrates methods of bringing the ball under control (15 minutes; color; 1975). Brigham Young University, Educational Media Center, 290 Herold R. Clark Building, Provo, Utah 84602.

Soccer: Key Factors in Defense Play. Demonstrates defensive support, tackling and kicking (16 minutes; b & w; 1972). Indiana University, Audio Visual Center, Bloomington, Indiana 47401.

Soccer: Pass, Dribble, Shoot. Analyzes passing, dribbling, and shooting. Uses stop-action photography for several types of kicking (11 minutes; color; 1970). University of Wisconsin/Madison, Bureau of Audio-Visual Instruction, 1327 University Avenue, Madison, Wisconsin 53706.

Soccer: Shooting and Using the Instep. Discusses critical aspects of goal shooting and passing (15 minutes; color; 1974). Brigham Young University, Educational Media Center, 290 Herold R. Clark Building, Provo, Utah 84602.

questions and answers

MULTIPLE CHOICE

1. The game of soccer is played in more than _____ nations.
   a. 80   b. 100   c. 110   d. 130   (p. 3)

2. Within recent years the popularity of soccer in the United States has
   a. increased tremendously   c. decreased slowly
   b. remained the same   d. decreased rapidly   (p. 3)

3. A volley kick is executed when the ball is
   a. rolling on the ground
   b. stationary on the ground
   c. at least as high as the head
   d. in the air, either before or after it bounces   (p. 11)

4. The instep kick is
   a. mainly used for short passes
   b. used when both power and accuracy are needed
   c. less effective when the ball is bouncing
   d. is not a skill pertaining to soccer   (p. 10)

5. The inside of the foot kicks are good for short passes, but they
   a. are not too deceptive
   b. lead to lack of ball control
   c. encourage bunching up the players
   d. lead to tripping and stumbling over the ball   (p. 13)

6. Which of the following statements related to kicking is *incorrect?*
   a. Keep your eyes on the ball at all times.
   b. Your body should be relaxed, especially the kicking leg.
   c. Practice kicking on a fast moving ball.
   d. Know the direction and distance you want the ball to travel.   (p. 10)

7. When performing the flick or jab, you should try to _____ the ball with the outside of the foot.
   a. kick   b. jab   c. loft   d. deflect   (p. 13)

8. Which of the following statements concerning dribbling is *correct?*
   a. Kick rather than push or tap the ball.
   b. Work for speed rather than ball control.
   c. Keep the ball near the feet throughout the dribble.
   d. Swerving, feigning, and change of pace make dribbling much less effective.
   (p. 20)

9. The process of bringing the ball under your control is called
   a. charging   b. dribbling   c. passing   d. trapping   (p. 16)

10. When executing the stomach or chest trap, you should
    a. jump off both feet and allow your body to "give"
    b. cover the abdomen or chest with your arms
    c. jump toward the ball with the body rigid
    d. flex one knee, raising the foot off the ground three to four inches   (p. 18)

11. Which of the following statements concerning passing is *incorrect?*
    a. The passer must be sure the ball can be passed without being intercepted.
    b. Accuracy is of little importance if the ball is kicked skillfully.
    c. The passer should pass only to an unmarked teammate.
    d. The passer must be able to kick the ball with enough skill so that the receiver can gain control of it.   (p. 19)

12. A good method of gaining control of a ball in low flight is the
    a. half-volley kick
    b. chest trap
    c. stomach trap
    d. inside of the thigh trap   (p. 18)

13. The outside of the foot dribble
    a. increases the speed of the dribbler
    b. is easy to execute
    c. increases ball control
    d. reduces the speed of the dribbler   (p. 21)

14. A tackle is considered successful if you
    a. physically drag your opponent to the ground
    b. knock your opponent off balance
    c. take the ball from your opponent by use of the feet
    d. tag your opponent with one hand between the shoulders and knees
    (p. 24)

15. Which of the following is essential to safety when heading the ball?
    a. Push off or climb up your opponent whenever possible.
    b. Never head a ball lower than waist height.
    c. Charge your opponent while he is in the air heading the ball.
    d. Be the first to head the ball, regardless of its height, if you expect to gain control of it.   (p. 23)

16. The pivot instep kick is used for _____ balls.
    a. bouncing   b. high fly   c. low fly   d. ground   (p. 12)

17. Positional play for fullbacks requires that these players
    a. remain in their own half of the field to help protect the goal area
    b. remain directly opposite each other at all times
    c. assist the forwards in scoring attempts
    d. avoid entering the goal area since they cannot use their hands   (p. 44)

18. If, as a fullback, you cover the goal for the goalie, you
    a. have the same privileges as the goalie
    b. must remain in the goal box in order to handle the ball
    c. cannot touch the ball with your hands
    d. may catch the ball, but you cannot run with it.   (p. 45)

19. Because of the position of play, the _____ has the best opportunity for directing the team's defense.
    a. right fullback   c. left fullback
    b. goalie   d. center halfback   (p. 44)

20. Positional play for the right and left halfbacks requires that these players
    a. remain directly opposite each other at all times
    b. assist the forwards in scoring attempts
    c. remain in their own half of the field to help protect the goal area
    d. follow up attempted goal shots in an effort to get a second try for a goal
                                                                (p. 46)

21. The goalkeeper has the privilege of using the hands to play the ball
    a. anywhere in the field of play
    b. anywhere outside the penalty area
    c. within the penalty area only
    d. only when the fullbacks are outside the penalty area   (p. 44)

22. Good goaltending implies that the goalkeeper should
    a. remain on the goal line to be sure that the ball does not cross it
    b. leave the goal unguarded, if necessary, to assist the fullbacks
    c. remain within the goal box at all times
    d. slowly move out in front of the goal box to pick up a potential scorer
                                                                (p. 44)

23. This player, by playing a waiting game, can distract the opponent and be fresh as the attack gets underway.
    a. center forward   c. outside right
    b. inside right   d. center halfback   (p. 47)

24. One of the main types of offense in soccer is the
    a. player-for-player defense   c. set offense
    b. long passing game   d. dribbling offense   (p. 50)

25. The _____ is in the best position to direct the attack.
    a. outside right   c. left halfback
    b. center forward   d. center halfback   (p. 46)

26. Because of their position of play, the _____ can use dribbling to a distinct advantage.
    a. inside forwards   c. outside forwards
    b. halfbacks   d. fullbacks   (p. 48)

27. The outside forwards
    a. must be able to stay with or ahead of the ball at all times
    b. play a waiting game so they are fresh when the attack gets underway
    c. act in the capacity of playmakers
    d. are usually responsible for throw-ins   (p. 48)

28. Defensively, the inside forward must mark the opposing
    a. fullback   c. center forward
    b. outside forward   d. halfback   (p. 48)

29. In the three-back system, one of the major responsibilities of the third back is
    a. directing the attack
    b. providing a decoy
    c. setting up plays
    d. assisting on defense   (p. 49)

30. Regardless of the type of offensive formations used, the offense should **never**
    a. carry the attack on a wide front so as to spread out the defense
    b. switch the play from one side of the field to the other by crossing the ball
    c. attack in a straight line across the field as the penalty area is approached
    d. use backward passes in an effort to keep the defense off guard.   (p. 51)

31. Which of the following statements concerning defensive strategy is most correct?
    a. Avoid passing the ball to the goalkeeper when pressed by the attackers.
    b. The more spread out the defense, the more vulnerable it is.
    c. Avoid arranging the defense in depth or waves.
    d. When a retreat is necessary, retreat quickly in order to set up your defense.
                                                                          (p. 53)

32. The player-for-player defense requires that each member of the team marks
    a. a particular opponent throughout defensive situations
    b. the player with the ball in a specified area
    c. the player with the ball when in his or her half of the field
    d. the player with the ball in the opponent's half of the field   (p. 53)

33. Early English aristocrats disliked the game of soccer because
    a. their teams were easily defeated by the teams of the common people
    b. it required considerable expensive equipment which the common people
       could not afford
    c. inadequate rules and poor organization led to loss of life and destruction of
       property
    d. it interfered with their leisure-time sports such as hunting and gambling
                                                                          (p. 4)

34. The emblem of world supremacy in soccer is the
    a. Davis Cup
    b. World Cup
    c. Stanley Cup
    d. National Open Challenge Cup   (p. 5)

35. The corner kick provides an excellent opportunity for scoring since
    a. the ball must be kicked toward the mouth of the goal
    b. this kick is the same as an indirect free kick
    c. the ball is put into play by the defending team
    d. a goal may be scored directly from it   (p. 53)

36. Many historians consider the _____ version of soccer to be the origin of
    the game we play today.
    a. English   b. Roman   c. Greek   d. Persian   (p. 4)

37. Which of the following stipulations governing the kickoff is *incorrect*?
    a. Before the ball is kicked, all players must be in their respective halves of
       the field.
    b. Players of the opposing team must be outside the center circle until
       the ball is kicked.
    c. The player who kicks the ball may dribble if the official is notified before
       hand
    d. After a proper kickoff, the ball can be kicked in any direction by any player.
                                                                          (p. 55)

38. The change in the game of soccer that distinguished it from football was
    a. aerial passing
    b. the shape of the ball
    c. the number of players on the team
    d. running with the ball   (p. 4)

39. The governing body of American soccer today is the
    a. United States Soccer Football Association
    b. Intercollegiate Soccer Football Association
    c. United States High School Soccer Association
    d. Federation Internationale de Football Association   (p. 5)

40. All opposing team members must remain _____ yards from the ball for free kicks.
    a. five   b. ten   c. fifteen   d. twenty   (p. 58)

41. The official should call the ball out of play when it
    a. touches any out-of-bounds line
    b. strikes a goalpost, crossbar, or corner flag
    c. is in bounds and is kicked by a player who is out-of-bounds
    d. is in the air and passes out of play, but returns to the field of play   (p. 56)

42. On the kickoff, the ball is dribbled by the player who kicks the ball. In this instance
    a. there is no violation of the kickoff rule
    b. the kick is retaken by the offending team
    c. an indirect free kick is awarded to the opposing team
    d. a direct free kick is awarded to the opposing team   (p. 56)

43. When the defensive team deliberately commits a foul in its own penalty area, the offended team is awarded a
    a. goal kick   c. corner kick
    b. penalty kick   d. direct free kick   (p. 58)

44. Which of the following is not an offense for which a direct free kick is given?
    a. handling the ball   c. charging violently
    b. jumping at an opponent   d. unsportsmanlike conduct   (p. 57)

45. A kick from which a goal cannot be scored directly is classified as
    a. an indirect free kick   c. a direct free kick
    b. a corner kick   d. a penalty kick   (p. 57)

46. The most important piece of equipment for a soccer player is the
    a. eye protector   c. stocking
    b. shoe   d. headgear   (p. 62)

47. The penalty for jumping into the air while executing a throw-in is
    a. an indirect free kick
    b. a direct free kick
    c. a throw-in awarded to the opposing team
    d. a severe warning by the official   (p. 59)

48. A kick taken from within the quarter-circle at a corner flag post is called a
    a. goal kick   c. free kick
    b. penalty kick   d. corner kick   (p. 60)

49. Courtesy and sportsmanship in soccer imply that you
    a. develop emotional control
    b. give up aggressive play
    c. criticize your opponent and the officials only when they can't hear you
    d. give up the will to win   (p. 61)

50. Internationally _____ is considered to be the finest soccer player.
    a. Eusebio   b. Torres   c. Pelé   d. Sandro   (p. 63)

51. The ability of the whole body, or part of it, to apply force defines
    a. strength   b. tonus   c. endurance   d. fatigue   (p. 39)

52. The alignment of players when using the four-back system is
    a. 4-3-4   b. 4-1-6   c. 4-2-4   d. 4-3-3   (p. 50)

53. The number of fans who listened to or watched the 1978 World Cup Championship is estimated at
    a. one billion
    b. one hundred thousand
    c. one million
    d. five billion   (p. 5)

54. According to women's rules, the sliding tackle is considered an attempt to _____ the opponent.
    a. charge
    b. trip
    c. strike
    d. hold   (p. 25)

55. Immediately after fielding the ball, as goalie you should
    a. fall upon it
    b. hold it up over your head
    c. bring it into your chest
    d. hold it to one side of your body   (p. 28)

TRUE OR FALSE

56. The fact that soccer is often called the "universal" game is misleading since only a relatively few countries play the game.   (p. 3)

57. The game of soccer, unlike most games played in the United States, is played primarily with the feet.   (p. 1)

58. To perform the push pass, place the inside of the foot slightly under the ball and lift as you kick.   (p. 13)

59. To execute the instep kick correctly, the toe of the shoe should contact the ball slightly below its midpoint.   (p. 11)

60. The sole of the foot trap can be used to trap a rolling or bouncing ball.
                                                                  (p. 16)

61. When passing the ball, you should look at the ball while in the act of kicking.
                                                                  (p. 20)

62. A simple rule to follow is dribble the ball whenever possible rather than pass.
                                                                  (p. 20)

63. The throw-in is important because it is a method of restarting play and initiating offensive play.   (p. 21)

64. When executing the pivot instep kick, the forward swing of the kicking leg is initiated in the hip.   (p. 12)

65. When executing the throw-in, you may use one hand to throw the ball so long as the ball is delivered from over the head.   (p. 21)

66. When executing the outside of the foot dribble, the ball is dribbled with the same foot every other step.   (p. 20)

67. The sole of the foot and heel kicks are easier to perform if the ball is rolling and you are running.   (p. 15)

68. In order to head the ball effectively, it is important to wait for the ball with both feet firmly placed on the ground. (p. 23)

69. Practice of correct movements is basic to learning soccer skills, but perfection depends upon more than mere repetition. (p. 33)

70. When charging, you must hold your arms away from the body and have both feet on the ground. (p. 23)

71. Two dangerous situations that fullbacks should avoid are dribbling and passing in front of the goal. (p. 45)

72. The center forward is primarily an offensive player. (p. 47)

73. On defense, the center half marks the opposing center half. (p. 46)

74. An important point concerning throw-in plays is to throw the ball to the feet of all teammates except the goalkeeper. (p. 52)

75. Generally the inside forwards kick all corner kicks. (p. 48)

76. A well-devised kickoff play consists of a long kick deep into the opponent's territory. (p. 52)

77. A type of soccer called Harpaston was played by the ancient Greeks. (p. 4)

78. The first intercollegiate soccer game played in America was between Rutgers and Princeton. (p. 4)

79. The fact there are presently no professional soccer leagues in the United States is the main reason for lack of interest and enthusiasm in the game. (p. 5)

80. The attacking team can score a goal by using any portion of the arms from the elbow to the shoulder. (p. 56)

81. Within the United States, soccer's most coveted award is the National Open Challenge Cup. (p. 5)

82. Basically, the offside rule eliminates the possibility of a player remaining close to the goal area where a goal can be scored from short range. (p. 56)

83. When a penalty kick has been awarded, the goalkeeper must stand stationary on the goal line until the ball is kicked. (p. 58)

84. The touchline is the line that divides the field into two equal halves. (p. 7)

85. The round-robin type of tournament is popular in a great many American schools and colleges. (p. 9)

86. Even though the sliding tackle forces the tackler to the ground, beginning players should master this skill as quickly as posible.. (p. 25)

87. The fact that soccer is a team game makes it impractical for two or three students to practice game skills and strategies. (p. 38)

88. Students participating in the game of soccer must be willing to anticipate dangerous situations that can lead to injury. (p. 42)

89. Within the last few years interest in soccer in the United States has been decreasing. (p. 5)

90. Regardless of the method of clearing the ball, the goalie should first move to either side of the goal area. (p. 31)

91. Beginning goalies should punch the ball sideward and downward.   (p. 30)

92. The goalie should learn to dive for the ball from a kneeling position before attempting it from a standing or running position.   (p. 30)

93. According to men's rules, protection of the chest is *not* considered handling the ball.   (p. 60)

94. According to women's rules, a direct free kick is awarded for *attempting* to trip, kick, strike, or jump at an opponent.   (p. 60)

COMPLETION

95. To kick a fast, low-curved ball with sideward spin you would use the _____ of the foot kick.   (p. 11)

96. The volley kick will yield a _____ ball, while the half-volley will produce a _____ ball.   (p. 12)

97. A _____ is considered successful when you have intercepted the ball and are ready to play it.   (p. 16)

98. The only player who would not use the side of the foot trap is the _____ .   (p. 17)

99. The type of dribble that gives best ball control is the _____ of the foot dribble.   (p. 20)

100. A ball that goes out of play over a touchline is put into play by means of a _____ .   (p. 7)

101. When attempting to keep your body between an opponent and the ball, you should use the _____ of the foot dribble.   (p. 20)

102. To head the ball forward, the ball should make contact with the _____ .   (p. 23)

103. To improve retention, it is important to learn not only the how of motor skills but also the _____ and _____ .   (p. 33)

104. The primary position of play for the goalie is the _____ (p. 44)

105. Two of the most useful kicks for fullbacks are the _____ and _____ .   (p. 45)

106. When playing the halfback position, you should force the dribbler to the _____ of the field.   (p. 46)

107. When the goal kick is taken from your own goal, the _____ generally kicks the ball.   (p. 52)

108. The _____ type of defense is recommended for beginning players since it stresses positional play.   (p. 53)

109. In the three-back system, the loss of the center halfback will _____ the area to be covered by the other halfbacks.   (p. 49)

110. When the referee holds the ball and lets it fall to the ground between two opponents, it is called a _____ .   (p. 6)

111. Major infractions of rules and personal misconduct are offenses for which a _____ free kick is given.   (p. 57)

112. The _____ , who is usually responsible for throw-ins, should develop accuracy in throwing the ball. (p. 46)

113. When an offensive player kicks the ball over the goal line, but fails to score a goal, a _____ kick is awarded. (p. 59)

114. The side of the foot volley is used when the ball is approximately _____ high or lower. (p. 12)

115. The only way to increase strength and endurance is by means of the _____ _____ . (p. 39)

116. The three-back system is an effective defense against the _____ offense. (p. 49)

117. The four-back game utilizes one of the _____ as the fourth fullback. (p. 49)

118. The length and width of the official women's soccer field are _____ _____ than the length and width of the official men's soccer field. (p. 3)

119. For the goalie there are basically _____ types of balls to field in soccer. (p. 28)

120. When the goalie deflects the ball over the crossbar or to the sides of the uprights by means of finger and wrist movements, it is referred to as _____ the ball. (p. 29)

ANSWERS TO SOCCER EVALUATION QUESTIONS

Page	Answer
6	The last World Cup was won by Argentina in 1978. The competition will be held again in 1982. (p. 5)
11	Skill question, no answer
12	Skill question, no answer
14	Skill question, no answer
18	Turn the foot outward for an inside of the foot trap and inward for an outside of the foot trap. (p. 17)
20	Skill question, no answer
21	Aim ahead of the receiver so that the player can be moving forward as the ball comes within reach. (p. 22)
22	Head the ball to score a goal, to pass to a teammate, or to ground the ball (p. 23)
23	Skill question, no answer
27	The goalkeeper should try to place himself/herself directly in front of the approaching ball. (p. 27)
34	Skill question, no answer
36	Skill question, no answer
40	Skill question, no answer

43   By advancing, the goalkeeper narrows the angle through which a goal may be scored. (p. 44)

45   The left fullback should move toward the center of the field while remaining well behind the advancing right fullback. (p. 45)

47   The center halfback marks the center forward; the right halfback, the inside left; the left halfback, the inside right. (p. 46)

50   The four-back system places the heaviest demands on the forwards and was designed to be used against a four offense attack. The three-back defense is effective against the W offense. (pp. 49-50)

50   B is in a poor position to receive the ball; A failed to pass ahead of the receiver; A has passed to a guarded teammate. (pp. 19-20)

52   The short-passing attack provides good ball control and fewer interception possibilities under the conditions described. (p. 50)

53   X_2, as goalkeeper, should move to one side of the goal area and clear the ball with either a long accurate throw or a long hard kick. A_1 should follow up the shot into the goal area. Y_2 should be ready to move in to goal area if needed there, and Z_2 should move out ready to receive pass from X_2 or play of Y_2 and Z_2 may be reversed.

57   If the goalkeeper leaves the penalty area, he may be charged. (p. 57)

59   Neither A nor B is offside. There were two opponents nearer the goal than A when the ball was played. B is not offside because the ball was played before it touched the opponent, X_2. (p. 56)

QUESTION ANSWER KEY

Multiple Choice

1.	d	12.	d	23.	a	34.	b	45.	a
2.	a	13.	a	24.	b	35.	d	46.	b
3.	d	14.	c	25.	d	36.	a	47.	c
4.	b	15.	b	26.	c	37.	c	48.	d
5.	a	16.	d	27.	a	38.	d	49.	a
6.	c	17.	a	28.	d	39.	a	50.	c
7.	b	18.	c	29.	d	40.	b	51.	a
8.	c	19.	b	30.	c	41.	d	52.	c
9.	d	20.	b	31.	b	42.	c	53.	a
10.	a	21.	c	32.	a	43.	b	54.	b
11.	b	22.	d	33.	c	44.	d	55.	c

True or False

56.	F	64.	T	72.	T	80.	F	88.	T
57.	T	65.	F	73.	F	81.	T	89.	F
58.	F	66.	T	74.	T	82.	T	90.	T
59.	F	67.	F	75.	F	83.	T	91.	F
60.	T	68.	F	76.	F	84.	F	92.	T
61.	T	69.	T	77.	T	85.	T	93.	F
62.	F	70.	F	78.	F	86.	F	94.	T
63.	T	71.	T	79.	F	87.	F		

Completion

 95. outside
 96. lofting—or a synonym
 97. trap
 98. goalkeeper
 99. inside
100. throw-in
101. outside
102. forehead or hairline
103. why/when
104. penalty area
105. volley/half-volley
106. outside
107. goalkeeper

108. zone
109. increase
110. drop ball
111. direct
112. halfback
113. goal
114. knee
115. overload principle
116. W
117. wing halfbacks
118. less—or a synonym
119. three
120. tipping

index